"*This book is a wonderful source of insight and understanding from someone who knows firsthand the transformative powers of the brain's plasticity.*"

- Dr. Michael Merzenich, world authority on brain plasticity and author of *Soft-Wired: How the New Science of Brain Plasticity Can Change Your Life.*

"*Debbie Hampton gives a behind the scenes look at the workings of the mind and brain, and draws from some of the leading scientists and teachers of our time. But more than that, she weaves her own powerful story of recovery from brain injury into each chapter. She provides a refreshing and personal look into mindfulness, neuroplasticity and recovery from someone who has travelled the journey. A remarkable book that is beautifully written, compassionate and wise.*"

- Dr. Sarah McKay, neuroscientist, writer, and founder of *Your Brain Health.*

"*Absolutely the best book of its type I have ever read. Highly recommend.*"

- Linda R. Harris, reader

"*This book has changed my attitude to my life and there are very few books around that possess this potential. Debbie Hampton's vivid, humorous, unsentimental and intimate writing style, her own tragic personal experience and the hardcore scientific discoveries that she refers to throughout are what makes this a book I would strongly recommend to anyone who has ever been troubled by depression or anxiety.*"

- Jennifer Sundberg, reader

Beat Depression and Anxiety By Changing Your Brain

With Simple Practices That Will Improve Your Life

Debbie Hampton

Please visit
thebestbrainpossible.com
for more information and inspiration.

ISBN-13: 978-1514112007
ISBN-10: 1514112000

Table of Contents

Who Am I To Be Telling You Anything

The short answer is: I'm someone who has done it. I'm not a doctor or therapist. BUT...I've been there — in that deep dark hole of depression, riddled with anxiety, and feeling like there was no air to breathe and no way out.

After taking care of my brother as he wasted away and died from AIDs, the end of my 18-year marriage to my high school sweetheart in an ugly parting that made *Divorce Court* look civil, and years of wrong turns, things not working out, and being flat-out disappointed with life, I tried to kill myself in June of 2007, by swallowing over 90 pills, mostly brain drugs. Because I wasn't found in time, the drugs went all the way through my system wreaking destruction. I woke up a week later from a coma with a serious brain injury to a very different world.

The brain injury forced me to make radical changes in my lifestyle and mindset that I'd needed to make long before. Better late than never! Because a lot of the underlying belief systems and perceptual foundation upon which I'd built my reality withered away along with brain cells, I got to start with a clean slate, so to speak.

Through years of daily effort and the practices covered in this book, I made a remarkable recovery and healed my life along with my brain. By consciously working with and altering my thoughts, behaviors, and emotions, I transformed my world which in turn, changed my physical brain and its default mode of operation.

Today, I live a brain healthy life incorporating daily practices to maintain the balance and happiness I've found. Although I still talk funny and have some slight manual dexterity issues, I'm better than ever.

Your brain is neuroplastic, meaning that its structure and function are literally, physically shaped by what you do repeatedly in your life – behaviors, emotions, and even thoughts – which works both for and against you. This book is about putting it to work to your benefit.

We have much more power to recover from depression, stop anxiety and worry, improve our brain's functioning, and create our own peace and happiness with the gray matter between our ears than ever thought possible. I did it. You can too! No brain injury required.

Chapter One

My Brain's Story

We cannot solve our problems, with the same thinking that we used when we created them.

Albert Einstein

Taking gulps of my favorite, cheap wine right out of the bottle, I quickly swallowed handful after handful of the happy-colored pills. They looked like candy, but there was no sweet taste going down. I knew that I wasn't supposed to mix meds with alcohol, but in this case, it didn't matter.

"That should do it," I thought as tears dripped off my chin. I considered making myself throw up. Being bulimic in college, I could've easily done it, but I didn't.

I felt calm - proud even - for having the guts to actually do it. Once the deed was done, the snarly witch in my mind finally shut up. The non-stop mental movie of the painful past and dreaded future reached the end of the reel at last, and it was eerily quiet inside my head for the first time in a long time.

It was a sunny spring morning in June of 2007, just like any other Wednesday morning, except this was the morning that I decided I wanted to die.

After taking the pills, hours went by before someone found me, and it was hours after that before what I'd taken became known. Because too much time had passed, my stomach wasn't pumped, and the drugs went all the way through my body, wreaking destruction. Needless to say, it wasn't a successful suicide attempt, but the overdose did land me in the hospital for two weeks and left me with a serious brain injury.

When I woke up from the coma that I'd been in for the past week, my speech was garbled, slurred, without inflection, and like my thinking, s-l-o-w. I had trouble controlling my bladder, couldn't coordinate breathing and swallowing anymore, my hands constantly shook while hanging limply at my sides when I walked, and my balance was off. I was severely mentally impaired and didn't know that my second son had been born, that my brother had died or that I had gotten divorced.

My short and long-term memories were nonexistent at first. I couldn't focus on anything for more than a few seconds, make sense of what I was seeing, or what was happening. It was as if someone had commandeered the remote control and was flipping through the channels inside my head. Before I could figure out what was in front of me, like acts of a play, new props and characters would invade the scene and change everything.

The closest thing I can liken my brain-injured state to is being out-of-your-mind drunk, but this time, I didn't sober up in a couple of hours.

After 43 years of living with pervasive fear, anxiety, self-doubt, and catastrophic and negative thinking, 11 years after taking care of and watching my brother die of AIDs, and three years after the end of my 18-year marriage to my high school sweetheart, I found myself a depressed, divorced, single mother who had no idea who she was or what she was doing here. I'd gotten so lost, removed from my own soul, and flat out disgusted and disappointed with life that I decided to end it all.

In the year following the brain injury, I naturally regained some memory, intelligence, physical coordination, speech, and motivation. I then used what wits I'd recovered to find out everything I could about healing my brain promising myself, "If I *have* to live, I *am not* living like this!" From the time I got out of bed until I hit the sheets again, my sole focus for years was rebuilding my brain. Little did I know that in the process of fixing my brain, I would also heal my life.

Partly because the brain injury made me a little OCD and partly because I'd always had the tendency, I was obsessively determined to recover. In addition to exercising daily to promote brain cell growth, I spent hours every day brain training and doing my own speech, manual dexterity, and other therapies to improve my brain processes. I adopted a brain healthy diet, guzzled water, took supplements, and got lots of sleep.

To overhaul the unhealthy thinking patterns that led to the suicide attempt, I began practicing mindfulness, gratitude, yoga, meditation, visualization, and thought reframing to build new, healthier pathways in my brain. While talk therapy hadn't proven successful for me in the past, I gave CBT (cognitive behavioral therapy) a try and found it life changing. It took years, but I did fully recover with a better-than-ever brain and mental and emotional intelligence I hadn't had before.

Although I never thought I'd say this when I was in the midst of the nightmare, the brain injury was a blessing in disguise because it forced me to make the changes I'd needed to make in my life long before. In rebuilding my brain, I took control of my mind, consciously directed my brain functioning and behavior, and completely turned my life around.

Whereas I used to cling to the bottom rung of the mental health ladder, I've climbed up to happily stand at the top. I like the view much better from here. I'm joyful, calm, optimistic, fulfilled, connected, and engaged in life. I told someone recently, "I don't feel like I'm searching for anything." That's a mighty nice feeling.

I know what you're probably thinking, "Oh yeah, life got better for her because her circumstances improved." My life is still far from what anyone would consider ideal. As I write this, my kids live in another state with their father who sued me for custody right after the suicide attempt. I have no significant other and haven't had a romantic relationship since the brain injury, and my financial future is anything but secure. Although it does sound pretty bad when spelled out like that, I'm happy and content.

Discovering the true power of my mind and learning to put it to work for me not only allowed me to heal from the brain injury, but also transform myself and my life from a mess to masterpiece. You can do it too.

Chapter Two

How Your Brain Makes Your Story

We do not see things as they are. We see things as we are.

Anais Nin

At the most basic level, your world is created by your brain. Making sense of the world and its happenings is nothing more than your brain's interpretation of the signals it receives as you go about your days just doing what you do interacting with your environment. Sound a little out there? Let me explain.

Color is nothing more than cone cells in your retina being stimulated by light waves within a certain range of the spectrum. Because each of our brains are different, our perceptions of color are different.

The sky is blue, right? No question.

However, your blue is going to be different than my blue. Maybe even very different. Neither is right or wrong. Both are blue. Your blue is just as blue to you as my blue is to me. Both are merely our individual brains making sense of the same signals. The words you hear are nothing more than air pressure waves hitting tiny hairs in your ear which take on the meaning your brain gives them. The understanding your brain assigns them is subjectively colored.

Each of us experience the world uniquely because our brains interpret the events and stimuli we encounter differently due to our physical brain function, memories, beliefs, and attitudes about ourselves, others, and the world shaped by family, religion, school, culture, and life encounters. These influences are typically below your conscious awareness, but determine how you respond to the world, interact in relationships, and think of and talk to yourself.

So, Mom and Dad, your sixth grade teacher, your best friend growing up and today, and your media intake all help paint your one-of-a-kind picture of reality.

Even your memory is subjective and colored by these subconscious shadows. Research has confirmed that our brains don't store everything verbatim like a computer and retrieve exact replicas. Our memories are re-creations. Your brain rebuilds a memory from a few key features and fills in the missing details based on associations and implicit and explicit knowledge. That's right! Your brain just makes it up, and you have no way of knowing what's recalled verbatim and what's constructed.

In his book, *Proust Was a Neuroscientist*, Jonah Lehrer writes "Our memories are not *LIKE* fiction. They ARE fiction." He compares memories to "a Xerox of a Xerox of a mimeograph of the original photograph."[1]

In your brain, a memory is made up of slight shifts in certain synapses firing in a specific sequence. Every time you recall a memory, the brain reconsolidates this process incorporating and filtering the thought through who you are and what you know at the time of remembering. Memory is an active and ongoing process, and according to Lehrer, "A memory is only as real as the last time you remembered it. The more you remember something, the less accurate the memory becomes."[2]

Because of our differing brains, each one of us really does live in our own little world. Reality depends on what actually happens (objective) and how your brain makes sense of what happens (subjective). Although there are many commonalities across all of our realities, it cannot be assumed that anything is the same for everyone or even remotely close to it.

Kind of freaky, right? But, wait! Here lies the superpower we all have. By purposefully effecting the variables determining your brain's interpretation of the world, you can change your brain and life for the better.

The key is to become conscious of and take control of your thoughts and mind. Remember that your brain factors in subconscious beliefs and attitudes about yourself, others, and the world when assigning meaning to incoming stimuli to create your reality. By becoming aware of your influences and consciously choosing which ones you buy into and allow to have impact, and intentionally inserting new ones, you can change your past and future and physically alter your brain.

Well, you can't literally change the past, of course. But by modifying your perspective and feelings about prior events, you differ their significance in your present life which allows you to modify your thoughts, behaviors, and future. However, your thoughts do literally change your brain's form and function. Pretty amazing, huh?! Let me tell you how.

Chapter Three

What Depression Looks Like In Your Brain

Depression is a prison where you are both the suffering prisoner and the cruel jailer.

Dorothy Rowe

A depressed or anxious brain looks just like any other brain. In fact, there's no brain scan, MRI, EEG or any other medical test that can definitively diagnose depression, and like many other brain disorders, it's not clearly understood. While we know the neurochemicals involved and many of the contributing factors, the truth is the experts really don't know the causes of depression or what's a cause and what's a symptom even.

At the most basic level, depression is just the routine activation of certain brain circuits, which everybody has, in specific patterns that result in depressive symptoms in that person.

In the book, *The Upward Spiral: Using Neuroscience to Reverse the Course of Depression, One Small Change at a Time*, Alex Korb explains depression like this:

> *The flow of traffic through a city is complex and dynamic – sometimes jamming up inexplicably and other times flowing smoothly, even at rush hour. The stock market and larger economy follow similar patterns as does the weather and even pop culture. Mathematically, these types of complex dynamic systems share many similarities, including the way the whole system — whether a traffic jam, a tornado, a recession or recovery, a viral tweet, or the next fad — can get caught in a runaway pattern: either an upward or downward spiral.*
>
> *So why do tornadoes happen in Oklahoma but not in New York? Because conditions are just right — the flatness of the land, temperature changes, humidity, and wind*

direction and speed. But there's nothing wrong with Oklahoma.

The same is true of your brain. In depression, there's nothing fundamentally wrong with the brain. It's simply that the particular tuning of neural circuits creates the tendency toward a pattern of depression. It has to do with the way the brain deals with stress, planning, habits, decision making, and a dozen other things — the dynamic interaction of those circuits. and once the pattern starts to form, it causes dozens of tiny changes throughout the brain that create a downward spiral.[1]

We're all born with the same basic brain structure, although the physical wiring, determining the activation of and communication between brain circuits, is unique to every person. The particular circuits excited over and over in your brain become the go-to default patterns for you and are the product of your thoughts, interactions with others and the world, and the events that happen to you throughout your life.

In the 1960s, we were told depression was because of a deficiency of the neurotransmitter norepinephrine. Then a theory, which is still popular, blamed depression on too little serotonin. Today, we know that it's much more complicated than either of these and involves many other neurochemicals which influence and are influenced by depression. (For example: dopamine, oxytocin, GABA, melatonin, endorphins, endocannaboids) To oversimplify, each neurotransmitter tends to contribute to a particular depressive symptom.

So, depression is just certain patterns of activated circuits in your brain and how they're impacting each other. It doesn't mean your brain is bad, is damaged goods, or not functioning properly. It means it has learned to operate in a way that results in depression.

How these tendencies take shape in your brain is multi-faceted, complex, and still somewhat of a mystery. But we do know that some of the factors which contribute to forming depressive patterns are:

1.   **Genetics**

Genes aren't your destiny by any means, but they do guide the initial development of your brain circuitry, and you can inherit a brain that's more likely to become depressed. Research has determined that there's a genetic component to depression and that as much as 40% of people with depression have a genetic link. If a person has a parent or sibling that has had major depression, they're three times more likely to develop the condition which may be both hereditary and environment. Women have a 42% chance of hereditary depression, while men only have a 29% chance.

2.   **Early Childhood**

Your childhood experiences literally shape your brain. While genes supply the basic blueprint for brain architecture, experience tweaks the brain circuitry development, and young brains are particularly sensitive. Stressful or traumatic events in childhood and adolescence guide the growth of neural connections and influence the levels of chemicals released in the brain which have powerful and lasting effects. The prefrontal cortex of the brain doesn't even finish maturing until a person is in their twenties and is susceptible to being shaped by stress the whole time.

3.   **Stress**

The current level of stress in your life is a big factor affecting which circuits are activated in your brain and can disrupt someone's good-for-your-brain behaviors starting their brain on a downward slide. For example, stress at work leads to working longer hours, which leads to missing exercise and yoga for weeks and not hanging out with friends or having much time for your partner, which puts you in a funk and causes troubles in the relationship which only leads to more stress which means losing sleep and binge eating etc.... You get the idea. Recent research has also shown that chronic high stress kills neurons and prevents the birth of new brain cells in a region called the hippocampus, which is necessary for a healthy stress response. (More on stress in Chapter 11)

4.   **Social Support**

We are social animals who need each other and are meant to be around other people. Many studies have shown that close relationships help protect a person from depression. In research, low self-rated social support was associated with higher levels of anxiety and depression. In another study involving depressed college students, lack of perceived social support, depicted as feeling unappreciated, unloved and uninvolved with family and friends, proved to be one of the most powerful predictors of persistent suicidal thoughts, even in the absence of any other risk factors.

5.   **Luck** (or lack of it)

Yes, randomness plays a part here. Korb writes:

> *That might be hard to hear, but it's true. Complex systems, like your brain, are influenced by tiny fluctuations. This explains why on some days there's a traffic jam and on other days cars flow smoothly. It explains why some YouTube videos go viral, and others remain in obscurity. And it explains why you feel great on some days and crappy on others....*[2]

Every brain has depressive tendencies and the potential to become depressed. But, the good news is every brain has wellness tendencies too. Just as a small change can start a brain spiraling down into depression, even a small shift can alter the balance, have a major impact, and begin an upward spiral.

Korb explains:

> *Changing the timing of a single stoplight may cause or prevent a traffic jam. A YouTube video may go viral from a single tweet. And sometimes tweaking the tuning of one brain circuit can start to reverse the course of depression.*[3]

Chapter Four

How Happy Happens In Your Brain

The stakes are very high when it comes to letting your brain use you. But, if you start to use it instead, the rewards are unlimited.

Deepak Chopra and Rudolph Tanzi in Super Brain

Your experience of your journey through life boils down to the chemicals in your brain. Happy, sad, mad, anxious, you name it. It can all be traced to what's going on inside your head. Your brain cooks up a chemical soup which controls your behavior, always instinctually encouraging you to seek out pleasure and avoid pain to try to ensure your survival. When your brain feels successful (whatever that means to your individual brain), you get rewarded with happy.

Rather than being in the passenger's seat in this process, science has proven without a doubt that you can take control of the wheel, affect the balances in your brain, and hack into your happy neurochemicals. By understanding how these chemicals originate and function, you can work experiences into your daily life to increase them to up your happiness, productivity, and peace of mind.

Dopamine

Dopamine motivates you to take action and encourages the persistence required to meet your needs, seek rewards, or approach goals - whether it's a college degree, a sugar fix, the next level in a video game, a strong drink, or money to pay the bills. The anticipation of the reward is actually what triggers a dopamine good feeling in your brain causing it to release the energy you need to move towards your goal. Then, you get another pleasure hit when you successfully meet the need.

You can stimulate the good feeling of dopamine by embracing a new goal and breaking it down into bite-size chunks, rather than only allowing your brain to celebrate when you hit the finish line. The idea is to create a series of small successes which keeps the dopamine flowing. And it's important to actually celebrate every accomplishment - buy that gadget you've been wanting or head to your favorite restaurant whenever you meet an interim goal. To avoid letting your dopamine lag, set new goals for yourself before achieving your current one.

The repetition of pursuing a good-for-you reward will build a new dopamine pathway in your brain until it's robust enough to compete with a dopamine habit that you're better off without.

Oxytocin

You may be familiar with oxytocin, sometimes referred to as the cuddle hormone. Oxytocin is released through closeness with another person and helps create intimacy and trust and build healthy relationships. Skin to skin contact releases oxytocin, for example a person gets a big hit during sex and mothers do during childbirth and breastfeeding. The cultivation of oxytocin increases fidelity and is essential for creating and maintaining strong bonds and improved social interactions.

However, you can boost oxytocin in other ways besides cuddling - your co-workers might not appreciate that too much. The release of oxytocin can also be triggered through social bonding, like eye contact and attentive conversation. A simple way to get an oxytocin surge is to give or get a hug. (You kind of have to do both at the same time, huh?) Also, research has shown that when someone receives a gift or just snuggles with their dog, oxytocin levels rise.

In today's cyber world, when we're often alone together on our digital devices, it's more important than ever to get some real face-to-face time and connect in-person within your community. Working out at a gym, attending social events, or having lunch with a friend is a great way to sustain these important human bonds and release oxytocin.

When someone betrays your trust, your brain releases unhappy chemicals which pave neural pathways telling you to withhold trust and oxytocin in the future. You may have to build trust again consciously to stimulate oxytocin by creating realistic expectations that both parties can meet. And each time the expectations are met, your brain rewards you with oxytocin and rebuilds your oxytocin circuits.

Serotonin

Serotonin plays so many different roles in your body that it's really tough to nail it down, but generally it can be thought of as the confidence molecule and flows when you feel significant or important and largely controls your overall mood. If you're in a good mood, you've got serotonin to thank. If you're in a bad mood, you've got serotonin to blame.

You enjoy the good feeling of serotonin when you feel respected by others, and your brain seeks more of that good feeling by repeating the behaviors that it learned triggered it in your past. The respect you got in your youth paved neural pathways that tell your brain how to get respect today.

Sometimes that drives people to seek attention in not-so-healthy ways that undermine their well-being and happiness in the long run. The solution to change this isn't to try to get rid of your brain's innate urge for status, because you need the serotonin. Instead, you can learn to develop your belief in your own worth and focus on your wins to provide the serotonin you need.

Loneliness and depression can appear when serotonin levels are low, although the connection here is not fully understood, and popular anti-depressants, called Serotonin-Specific Reuptake Inhibitors (SSRIs), alter the serotonin system in the brain. In various ways, SSRIs keep serotonin in the synaptic gap longer which was once thought to be a universal cure for depression. If that were true, these medications would work for everyone, which they don't. Some people don't respond to SSRIs, but do have success with medications that act on other neurochemical systems.

Reflecting on past significant achievements allows your brain to re-live the good experiences. In your brain, there's not much difference between real and imagined, and simply remembering a success produces serotonin. For this reason, gratitude and visualization practices work to actually change your brain for the better. If you need a serotonin boost during a stressful day, take a few moments to remember a past achievement or victory.

Also by getting some sunshine for 20 minutes, your skin absorbs UV rays, which promotes vitamin D and serotonin production. Interestingly, 80% of your serotonin exists in your gut, called the enteric nervous system, and is believed to play a role in mood, mental illness, and disease.

Endorphins

Endorphins have a chemical structure similar to opiates, serve to mask pain or discomfort, and are associated with the fight or flight response. Endorphins give you the oomph you need to help you power through any situation.

The word endorphin literally means "self-produced morphine," and conversely to what you might think, pain actually causes endorphins to be released. Similar to morphine, they act as an analgesic and sedative, diminishing your perception of pain.

You've probably heard of an "endorphin high." Well, a runner doesn't get that feeling unless they push their body to the point of distress. Endorphins helped our ancestors survive in emergencies, for example they could still run away when injured, but if you were on an endorphin high all the time, you would touch a hot stove or walk around on a broken leg.

Endorphins are produced during strenuous physical exertion, sexual intercourse, and orgasm. Laughing and stretching also cause the release of endorphins because both of these agitate your insides, causing moderate wear and tear and moderate endorphin flow. Studies have shown that just the anticipation of laughter increases endorphin levels. Researchers also report that acupuncture triggers endorphin production.

Oddly enough, smelling vanilla and lavender and eating chocolate and spicy foods has been linked with the production of endorphins.

When you have an idea of what's going on in your brain, you can begin to influence it to your benefit. You can stimulate more happy chemicals when you understand the job they evolved to do and what causes their release.

Your brain got wired from your individual past experiences, and the neurochemical patterns for every person are different. Each time your neurochemicals surged, your brain built connections and is wired now to turn on your brain chemicals in the same ways they were activated in the past.

When you're young, your brain is very changeable or neuroplastic (we'll talk lots more about this later) and neurons build new connections easily. As an adult, it's not as easy to build new circuits to turn on in new ways and requires a lot of repetition and focus. But it can be done. Your brain is capable of neuroplastic change until the day you die.

So, by picking a new happy habit and starting to implement it with repetition and consistency, you will begin shifting the neurochemical balance in your brain. Over time, your new happy habits will come to feel as natural to you as your old ones did.

Chapter Five

My Depression Is Not Your Depression

Walk a mile in my shoes, see what I see, hear what I hear, feel what I feel, THEN maybe you will understand why I do what I do. Until then, don't judge me.

Unknown

On my Best Brain Possible Facebook page, I've learned from experience to be very choosy about any posts on depression because people can get really passionate and colorfully expressive about THEIR depression. Many have strong opinions about whether the condition is based in biology, thinking, or lifestyle. Whenever I post an article about antidepressants, I find out really quickly that people either love them or hate them.

Recently, I posted the piece, Depression Doing The Thinking from *Psychology Today* (credible source, right?), explaining that:

> *One of the features of depression is pessimistic thinking. The negative thinking is actually the depression speaking. It's what depression sounds like. Depression in fact manifests in negative thinking before it creates negative affect.*[1]

A conversation with a fan followed that was basically, "nah nah nah nah, my depression is worse than your depression:"

> *Follower*: Depression is an illness not a behavior. This approach isn't much different than telling a depressed person to just snap out of it. Please don't contribute to perpetuating myths about mental illness.
>
> *Me*: Depression is a multi-faceted condition attributed to many things including thinking habits. Is all depression

just thinking? No. Is all depression biological? No. Please allow for both.

Follower: If that was directed at me, I don't need a lecture, thank you. I have suffered from depression for decades. there's a chance I know what I'm talking about. I appreciate, however, that it is very difficult for someone who doesn't suffer from a mental illness to understand what it's like. That's a large part of the challenge of breaking the stigma.

Me: I suffered from depression for decades and tried to commit suicide twice. So, does that make you or me an expert on depression? No! It makes you the expert on your depression and me the expert on mine. Every case is unique and different. I can't begin to know what is best or the solution for anyone else. All I can do is take care of myself, tell what worked for me, and share information. That's what I'm doing.

When writing my reply, I thought, "Really? Are we really going to get in a pissing match about whose depression is more legit?"

No one's depression is more real or more legitimate than anyone else's because no one's depression is the same as anybody else's. It's like comparing apples to oranges -- and grapes. You just can't do it.

Technically, depression is an umbrella term for many different conditions, behaviors, and symptoms. As explained in the last chapter, depression is a complex illness with a basis in brain neurochemicals and thought patterns with many other contributing factors such as life events, environment, biochemicals, and heredity.

Just as there's not a single definition or manifestation of depression, there's no one medical test to confirm a diagnosis. A diagnosis is a professional opinion based on clusters of symptoms exhibited and various test results. Lab tests are generally run to rule out other physical problems which may be causing the depressive symptoms, such as thyroid disease.

Although we may not all agree on what depression is exactly, I think we can all agree that depression is NOT just a matter of will. And, I don't think we can begin to decide what depression "should" look like, whose is worse, or what's the best treatment for someone else. We can only determine these things for ourselves.

While medications alone can and do help some people, others find success with mindfulness, affirmations, positive thinking, prayer, meditation, therapy, physical exercise, or by adding supplements or changing their diet.

After decades of taking antidepressants, I still tried to commit suicide. While healing the resulting brain injury, I cured my depression, maybe because I got my brain functioning right for the first time in my life or maybe it was because of all the other changes I made in my life. When I quit looking for an easy fix in a pill or therapist, and confronted and worked through my issues and altered my behaviors and thinking, the depression lifted and life got infinitely better as I grew stronger, more resilient, and positive.

Will the strategies that worked for me work for everyone? No. Each person has to find the right solution for them. Will making healthier food choices, exercising, and learning mental health tools make anyone's depression or anxiety worse? Undoubtedly not. Should options without the side effects and risks of medication be tried before resorting to antidepressants? IMHO, most definitely yes, except in urgent situations.

I have a friend who does yoga about every day, does cardio regularly, meditates, is a healthier eater than I am, and still doesn't find relief from her depression with all these practices. Does that make her depression more real than mine? No. It makes it different and more challenging to resolve.

For the record, there are generally nine recognized subsets of depression:

1.   **Major Depression** - extreme sadness, hopelessness, lack of energy, irritability, trouble concentrating, changes in sleep or eating habits, feelings of guilt, physical pain, and thoughts of death or suicide lasting for more than two weeks and usually recurring.

2. **Dysthmia** - low mood over a long period of time. People can function adequately, but not optimally. Symptoms include sadness, trouble concentrating, fatigue, and changes in sleep habits, and appetite.

3. **Postpartum Depression** - is characterized by feelings of extreme sadness, fatigue, loneliness, hopelessness, suicidal thoughts, fears about hurting the baby, and feelings of disconnect from the child after a woman gives birth.

4. **Seasonal Affective Disorder (SAD)** - usually starts in early winter and lifts in the spring, is likely due to a decrease in sunlight, and can be treated with light therapy. Symptoms include anxiety, increased irritability, daytime fatigue, and weight gain.

5. **Atypical Depression** - commonly includes a sense of heaviness in the arms and legs, like a form of paralysis, in addition to oversleeping and overeating. People with the condition may also gain weight, be irritable, and have relationship problems.

6. **Psychotic Depression** - is a mental state characterized by delusions and hallucinations. About 20% of people with depression have episodes so severe that they see or hear things that are not there.

7. **Bipolar Disorder** - is also called manic depressive disorder and has four subsets of its own. It consists of periods of extreme lows followed by periods of extreme highs.

8. **Premenstrual Dysphoric Disorder (PMDD)** - is a type of depression that affects women during the second half of their menstrual cycles and is more severe than PMS. Symptoms include depression, anxiety, and mood swings.

9. **Situational Depression** - is triggered by a stressful or life-changing event, such as job loss, the death of a loved one, trauma — even a bad breakup. Situational depression

tends to lift over time on its own, but can turn into major depression.

I want to say a few words about the stigma that goes with depression and anxiety. And if you think that it's bad, consider the stench around attempting suicide and having your children taken away. Holy mackerel! Talk about feeling embarrassed, ashamed, and judged.

I kept my suicide attempt a secret, as best as I could, and didn't talk about it for a long time after. It was a really hard thing to keep hidden because I couldn't hide the fact that I couldn't talk or was brain injured which always eventually led to the "What happened?" question. For a while, I just flat out lied.

Trying to keep a secret and feeling ashamed is its own kind of hell and torture. Goodness knows, I didn't need any more of that. I'd had enough of that bad stuff for a lifetime and figured out really quickly that if I was honest, putting the messy details right out there, that it took away any shame. (A large impetus for me was also that my ex-husband couldn't use it in court against me if I was honest about all of it.)

I have to admit that part of my being so forthcoming was the result of a brain injured mind which didn't know and wasn't constrained by the polite "shoulds" of society. I go back now and read blogs I wrote and think, "OMG! I told that!"

Eleanor Roosevelt said, "No one can make you feel inferior without your consent." It's so true, and I refuse to let shame be a part of my life. Instead, I extend compassion to the old Debbie and realize that she was doing the best she could with who she was at the time. I encourage you to be kind to yourself in the same way. Who deserves your compassion more than you?

Unfortunately, depression, anxiety, and suicide are very prevalent today. According to World Health Organization, worldwide as of 2014:

- *Over 800,000 people die by suicide every year.*
- *There is one death by suicide in the world every 40 seconds.*
- *Suicide is the second leading cause of death in the world for those aged 15-29 years.*
- *Depression is the leading cause of disability worldwide.*[2]

I've attempted suicide three times.

The first was when I was a junior in high school. After a break up with my boyfriend which was of monumental importance in my teenage world, I swallowed a bunch of aspirin, had my stomach pumped in the ER, and cheered at a football game later that night.

Fast forward two decades. I had now been married to the same boyfriend for 16 years and was a stay-at-home mom to two small sons. When the husband informed me that he wanted a divorce, I took off in my minivan, bought a six-pack of wine coolers, an assortment of over-the-counter pills, and a couple of bottles of the night-time-so-you-can-rest medicine. Parking the van in a remote corner of a 24-hour store lot, I downed it all and stretched out in the back seat to die.

Hours later, I woke in a panicked stupor and tried to drive home, but ploughed over a curb where I came to a stop, hung out of the door throwing up green goo, and passed out on the grass. Someone driving by called 911, and after being rushed to the ER and having my stomach pumped, I suffered no physical consequences, but did spend a couple of days in the psych ward of the hospital.

The last time, which you know about, was more serious — much more.

As part of my healing journey, I started talking and writing about my experiences and the touchy subjects of depression, suicide, and mental illness. When face-to-face, I noticed that the other person usually ended up acting like they felt awkward and embarrassed - not me - or they were compassionate and understanding. Many people went on to tell me their own stories about "having been there."

Not having open dialogues about these taboo topics only serves to perpetuate the negative cycle of mental illness, depression, and suicide. Mental health issues carry the stigma of shame, are hush-hushed, and people don't want to talk about these things because it makes *them* uncomfortable.

But we need to start talking about them. Depression, suicide, and mental illness affect everyone - most likely very intimately, at one time or another in their life. Instead of shaming and judging each other, isn't it time we started extending compassion and support to one another and began talking about mental health openly and honestly without fear or embarrassment?

Chapter Six

You're Not Stuck With The Brain You're Born With

Incredible change happens in your life when you decide to take control of what you do have power over instead of craving control over what you don't.

Steve Maraboli

The good news is your brain makes physical changes based on the repetitive things you do and experiences you have. The bad news is your brain makes physical changes based on the repetitive things you do and experiences you have. This capability of the brain to change itself, known as neuroplasticity, works both for you and against you.

Your brain is like Play-Doh minus the funky smell and is changeable and adaptable from cradle to grave. Neuroplasticity, a scientific truth of the last decade, is the ability of your brain to literally alter its physical structure and function through repeated thought, emotion, and activity.

It used to be believed that the adult brain was pretty much hardwired, but we now know that's not true. Not at all. Every single detail of which you are aware – sounds, sights, thoughts, feelings, and even that of which you aren't aware, unconscious mental and physical processes – can be directly mapped to neural activity in your brain which is constantly changing in response. What you pay attention to, think, feel, want, hope, and how you behave constantly sculpts your brain through experience-dependent neuroplasticity.

The neurological explanation of how this happens gets pretty complicated, but the basic concept is simple: every minute of every day you're shaping your brain for better or worse. In his book, *Just One Thing: Developing A Buddha Brain One Simple Practice At A Time*, Dr. Rick Hanson, neuropsychologist and Senior Fellow of the Greater Good Science Center at UC Berkeley, explains how neuroplasticity is accomplished:

1. Busy brain regions get more blood flow, since they need more oxygen and glucose.

2. The genes inside neurons get more or less active with the use of the neuron. For example, people who routinely relax have improved expression of genes that calm down stress reactions, making them more resilient.

3. Neural connections that are relatively inactive wither away; it's a kind of neural Darwinism, the survival of the busiest: use it or lose it.

4. "Neurons that fire together, wire together." This saying, from the work of Donald Hebb, means that synapses – the connections between neurons – get more sensitive, plus new neurons grow, producing thicker neural layers when fired repeatedly together. [1]

Neuroplasticity is an example of thought changing matter which, although remarkable, is no big deal for your brain. You can just think about your hand raising, and it does which is both extraordinary and very ordinary at the same time.

Neuroplasticity has allowed people who have had strokes and brain trauma to recover amazing functionality. Because of neuroplasticity, congenitally blind people's brains have figured out new ways to see, paralyzed limbs have become usable again, children with cerebral palsy have learned to move more smoothly, and children with autism have made cognitive strides once believed impossible. Experience-dependent neuroplasticity has also been harnessed to ease chronic pain, obsessive compulsiveness, worry, addictions, cravings, and depression. The examples go on and on.

There's a catch to neuroplasticity. It only happens when a person is paying attention and focusing on the input whether intentional or not. The same neuroplasticity that allows us to alter our brains and realities by implementing healthy, good-for-you habits conversely allows not-so-good habits to be unconsciously carved into our brains too. With directed attention, everyone has the ability to transform their brain and life for the better, but unfortunately, neuroplasticity is most often accomplished unconsciously etching bad habits into our brains. All bad habits, obsessions, and addictions are the result of neuroplastic change and can be reversed with the same process.

While self-directed neuroplasticity does work, it's not immediate or effortless and requires motivation, intention, and relentless, regular persistence. Research on neuroplasticity shows that intense focus is required to alter desired brain circuits and make new connections. Most neuroplastic change is incremental, not dramatic. Because neuroplasticity occurs for whatever's in your field of focused awareness, your attention is like a vacuum cleaner, sucking its contents into your brain. Directing your attention purposefully allows you to shape your brain and life over time.

Want to quit smoking? Interrupt the pattern habitually, and your brain will become your ally in the effort. Your brain can help you drop 10 pounds, end a drug addiction, stop biting your fingernails, quit worrying so much, put an end to living in fear, or stop negative self talk.

You can put your mind to work for you in just about any area of your life. Because nothing in the brain is hardwired, you can alter your behavior regularly, and in time your brain will make physical changes to reinforce the new pattern. Change your brain; change your life.

Neuroplasticity is the superpower you were born with. By adopting a brain healthy lifestyle and implementing practices to take control of your mind and thoughts, you can put neuroplasticity to work for you. Neuroplasticity does take time, persistence, and effort, but it does work and was key to my recovering from depression and a serious brain injury to find happiness and peace.

Although the science of neuroplasticity is still relatively new with unknown limits, having a malleable brain opens up a world of possibilities for us as individuals and as a society. Neuroplasticity has major implications for every aspect of human nature and culture including medicine, psychiatry, psychology, relationships, education, and more.

The bottom line is that we have grossly underestimated what our brains can do and the huge role they play in shaping our realities, lives, and happiness. Put neuroplasticity to work for you today, and you can change your brain and life for the better.

Chapter Seven

Negative Mental States Become Negative Brain Traits

There's a traditional saying that the mind takes the shape it rests upon; the modern update is that the brain takes the shape the mind rests upon.

Dr. Rick Hanson

If your mind regularly rests on worries, self-criticism, anger, and negativity, your brain will develop neural structures to support its companions: anxiety, low self-esteem, and reactivity because of neuroplasticity. Your brain has a natural negativity bias, which means it's always on the lookout for anything it deems bad, potential dangers or losses, to protect you. Although this hyper-vigilance helped our ancestors survive because more reactive, nervous, and clingy animals had better chances of passing on their genes, it doesn't do you much good in the present world.

This negative hair-trigger can activate when you're stuck in traffic, rushing to meet a work deadline, arguing with your partner, juggling taking care of the kids while fixing dinner and talking on the phone, or just reading the headlines leaving you anxious, stressed, and worried. When the slightest potential for trouble arises or the smallest thing goes wrong, your brain zeroes in on that one thing and minimizes everything else. If you get a glowing performance review from your boss, your brain will focus on the few constructive criticisms. Even though a first date goes well, you'll replay spilling your water at dinner over and over in your head. Can you relate?

Your brain perceives negative stimuli more rapidly and easily than positive because at one time, it could have meant the difference between life or death. We're programmed to recognize angry faces more quickly. We overestimate threats and underestimate opportunities. We over-learn from bad experiences and under-learn from good ones. In your brain, bad trumps good every single time. Eventually, unfavorable experiences snowball making you more sensitive to the negative and your brain more easily alarmed and reactive.

In his book, *Hardwiring Happiness: The New Brain Science of Contentment, Calm, and Confidence*, Rick Hanson writes, "One way or another, negative mental states can easily become negative neural traits." He continues:

> *Feeling stressed, worried, irritated, or hurt today makes you more vulnerable to feeling stressed, etc., tomorrow which makes you **really** vulnerable the day after that. Negativity leads to more negativity in a very vicious cycle.*[1]

This negativity bias gets etched into the physical structure of your brain as bad experiences get stored in implicit memory below conscious awareness and become the basis for how you feel and function. The contents of your implicit memory impact your life more than explicit memory, which is conscious, declarative knowledge.

Unless a positive experience is highly novel or intense, it usually has very little lasting effect on the brain. Hanson writes, "Your brain is like Velcro for negative experiences but Teflon for positive ones." Even though the brain's negativity bias is great for ensuring survival, it's lousy at promoting happiness, peace, fulfilling relationships, and long-term physical and mental health.

Being rooted in implicit memory made up of emotional wounds, fears, and doubts accumulated over your lifetime, the mental chatter in your head is mostly subconscious and critical or negative. Your subconscious core beliefs cause you to view the world as if you're wearing colored glasses without even realizing that you've got them on. You just believe the world is tinted that way because it's what you learned to believe. Because you interpret and interact with the world through these beliefs when your brain assigns meaning to incoming stimuli creating your reality, these core beliefs influence every experience you have.

By becoming aware of your filter, you can choose to take off your glasses and see the world differently. In order to minimize the influence of implicit garbage on your present reality, you have to first become aware of your thought patterns and core beliefs, especially those pesky ones that repeatedly pop into your head guiding your decisions and behavior, and notice which ones help you and which ones hold you back. Becoming aware of, interrupting, and redirecting your self talk to put it to work for you, instead of against you, can positively impact every aspect of your life and rewire your brain.

Once you're aware of your limiting beliefs, you can make your mind your ally in life by consciously choosing different thoughts that encourage and support you. Mary Englebreit said, "If you don't like something, change it; if you can't change it, change the way you think about it." An anonymous saying goes, "Life is like a kaleidoscope. Turn your head to a different angle to see it a whole new way."

Both of these quotes refer to your ability to choose your perspective in any situation. Every thought you have is subject to subconscious influence colored by your past, but you are not your thoughts. At any moment, you have the power to say, "Hey, wait a minute! That belief doesn't work for me anymore. I choose to look at it this way." By consciously changing your mindset in this way, with time and repetition, you can change your brain and life.

Chapter Eight

What's The Difference Between The Mind and Brain?

How did the scarecrow know he didn't have a brain?

Unknown

You know what your brain is, right? It's the three pounds of "convoluted mass of gray and white matter" in your head "serving to control and coordinate mental and physical actions."
OK. Now, define the mind. Not as easy, eh?!

You may be surprised to find that there's no single, agreed upon definition of the mind. The psychiatric, mental health, and medical professions each have their own functional definitions.
Equally surprising to me is that by default, a healthy mind is thought of as one with the absence of any symptoms of mental illness.
Really? I would hope it can get better than that.

Dr. Daniel Siegel, a professor of psychiatry at UCLA school of Medicine, co-director of the UCLA Mindfulness Awareness Research Center, and author of several books, teaches the concept of the Triangle of Well-Being to depict optimal mental health. He developed the concept into a field of study which has become known as interpersonal neurobiology.

He coined the term "mindsight" to describe the human capacity to perceive the mind of the self and others. On his website, Siegel writes about mindsight:

It is a powerful lens through which we can understand our inner lives with more clarity, integrate the brain, and enhance our relationships with others. Mindsight is a kind of focused attention that allows us to see the internal workings of our own minds. It helps us get ourselves off of the autopilot of ingrained behaviors and habitual responses. It lets us "name and tame" the emotions we are experiencing, rather than being overwhelmed by them[1]

It's common belief that the mind is the activity of the brain, but Siegel proposes that's only one part of it. On his "Triangle of Well-Being," each point of the triangle is an essential component of mental health.

One point is the physical brain and nervous system which are the mechanisms by which energy and information flow throughout our beings. Our senses take in information from the environment which become electrical signals traveling through the nervous system. The brain assigns meaning to these and responds by releasing neurochemicals and dispatching electrical signals regulating the body, controlling movement, and influencing emotions.

A second point on the Triangle of Well-Being is relationships, which are the means by which information and energy are shared. Part of your mind is made up of the energy and information flowing between and among people through spoken or written word. In person, this interchange also takes place through eye contact, facial expression, body language, posture, and gesture. In his book, *Mindsight: The New Science of Personal Transformation*, Siegel writes:

> *Our minds are created within relationships – including the one that we have with ourselves… each of us has a unique mind: unique thoughts, feelings, perceptions, memories, beliefs, and attitudes, and a unique set of regulatory patterns. These patterns shape the flow of energy and information inside us, and we share them with other minds.* [2]

The third point on the triangle is the mind, which is the process that regulates this flow of information and energy. Your mind observes and monitors the flow of energy and information across time while modifying it, giving it characteristics and patterns. In *Mindsight*, Siegel writes:

> *Consider the act of driving. To drive or "regulate" a car, you must both be aware of its motion and its position in space and also be able to influence how it moves. If you have your hands on the wheel but your eyes are shut (or focused on your text message), you can make the car move, but you*

are not driving it – because driving it means regulating the car's movement, its flow across time. If you have your eyes open but you're sitting in the backseat, you can monitor the movement of the car (and make comments, like one particular relative I know), but you can't actually modify its motion yourself. (no matter how hard you try, sorry.)[3]

Because of neuroplasticity, your brain creates new neural connections and grows neurons as each point on the triangle influences the others, and the flow of energy and information along the Triangle of Well Being moves in all directions. Your mind changes the structure of your brain and relationships. Your brain changes the structure of your mind and relationships, and relationships change your mind and brain.

Mindsight integrates the three parts of The Triangle of Well-Being to produce harmony which is mental health. Studies have shown that anyone can learn and develop mindsight, through mindfulness practices, leading to a better functioning brain, healthier mind, and happier, more vibrant, fulfilling life with enriched, satisfying relationships.

Sounds good to me!

Chapter Nine

The Difference Between Emotions And Feelings

Emotions play out in the theatre of the body. Feelings play out in the theatre of the mind.

Dr. Sarah McKay

Although the two words are used interchangeably, did you know that there are distinct differences between feelings and emotions?

Ok. Big deal.

Well, it kind of is a big deal because understanding the difference between the two can help you change unhealthy behaviors and find more joy and peace in your life. Feelings and emotions are two sides of the same coin and highly interconnected, but two very different things.

Emotions are lower level responses occurring in the subcortical regions of the brain, the amygdala and the ventromedial prefrontal cortices, creating biochemical reactions in your body altering your physical state. They originally helped our species survive by producing quick reactions to threat, reward, and everything in between arising in their environments. Emotional reactions are coded in our genes and while they do vary slightly individually and depending on circumstances, are generally universally similar across all humans and even other species. For example, you smile and your dog wags its tail.

The amygdala (there are two of them) aid in emotional arousal and also regulate the release of neurotransmitters necessary for memory consolidation which is why emotional memories can be so much stronger and longer-lasting. Emotions precede feelings, are physical, and instinctual. Because they are physical, emotions can be objectively measured by blood flow, brain activity, facial micro-expressions, and body language.

Feelings originate in the neocortical regions of the brain, are mental associations and reactions to emotions, and are subjective, being influenced by that subconscious stuff that colors everything: personal experience, beliefs, and memories. A feeling is the mental portrayal of what's going on in your body when you have an emotion and is the by-product of your brain perceiving and assigning meaning to the emotion. Feelings are the next thing that happens after having an emotion, involve cognitive input, usually subconscious, and cannot be measured precisely.

Feelings are sparked by emotions and colored by thoughts, memories, and images that have become linked with that particular emotion for you. But it works the other way around too. Just thinking about something threatening can trigger an emotional fear response. While individual emotions are temporary, the feelings they evoke may persist and grow over your lifetime. Because emotions cause subconscious feelings which in turn initiate emotions and so on, your life can become a never-ending cycle of painful and confusing emotions which produce negative feelings which cause more negative emotions without you ever really knowing why.

While basic emotions are instinctual and common to us all, the meanings they take on and the feelings they cause are individual based on your programming, past and present. Feelings are shaped by a person's temperament and experiences and vary greatly from person to person and situation to situation.

Your emotions and feelings play a powerful role in how you experience and interact with the world because they are the driving force behind many behaviors, helpful and unhelpful. It's possible to react to emotions and the feelings they evoke, guided by unconscious fear-based perceptions which you may not buy into anymore, yet you're living your life making decisions and behaving according to these out-dated beliefs. Living unaware like this almost always leads to problems and unhappiness.

By understanding the difference between and becoming aware of your emotions and feelings, determining which is which and their root causes, and then inserting conscious thought followed by deliberate action, you can begin to choose how you navigate and experience the world. Being able to do this can take you from being emotionally reactive to consciously responsive which can mean a calm rather than chaotic life.

Now, I don't mean to imply that by becoming aware of emotions and feelings that life will magically become filled with rainbows and unicorns. I'm suggesting that by learning the difference and changing your thinking and behavior, that no matter what's going on around you, you can maintain your balance, peace, purpose, and hope and move forward toward your goals.

In my marriage and in the years following the divorce, I learned to fear my ex-husband and his actions. After we split, just seeing an email from him pop up in my inbox would start my heart pounding; my breathing would become rapid and shallow, and I would actually begin to sweat. Soon, I would feel the accompanying dread, anxiety, and panic. My body was exhibiting the instinctual emotion of fear followed by the feelings I'd learned to associate with him.

In the past, I reacted from this fearful place as an overly emotional, angry victim who fought back. After the brain injury, I slowly matured emotionally, began to live more mindfully, and learned a different way to respond. It took years, but I was eventually able to not knee-jerk react and could consciously and deliberately choose my feelings and behaviors according to who I wanted to be and how I wanted to live my life. When I finally mastered this skill, life calmed way down for me, and I managed to find peace and happiness despite the fact that he continued his harassment.

While I was in the process of evolving, it would piss me off because my heart would still go crazy at just getting a message from him. I felt like my body was betraying me while, in my head, I knew better and stayed calm. My body was still emotionally reacting, but instead of letting it control me, I infused conscious thought and chose how I wanted to feel and proceed.

In the gaps between emotion, feeling, and acting, we all have the power to change and direct our lives for the better. Understanding your emotions and managing your feelings with conscious thinking so they don't hijack your brain followed up with conscious action can actually change your brain through neuroplasticity and change your life for the better.

Chapter Ten

Naming And Taming Worry And Anxiety

I've had a lot of worries in my life, most of which never happened.

Mark Twain

While worry and anxiety can both make you miserable, they are two distinct concepts occurring in different parts of your brain. You can have worry without anxiety, and anxiety without worry, but one often triggers the other, and they tend to be bosom buddies, unfortunately.

Worrying has become a national pastime. Whether you're worrying about paying your car loan, having job stability in an unstable economy or making sure your kid gets into college, there's never any shortage of material for mind sweat.

Worrying is thought based, occurs in your mind, and involves your thinking brain, the prefrontal cortex, interacting with the limbic system, which controls your basic emotions and instincts. The same circuits in your brain that make for super human intelligence: decision making, planning, and problem solving, also allow worry. So, when these parts are busy worrying, you can't use them for better things.

In your brain, the only difference between worrying and planning is the amount of emotional involvement and self-oriented processing in a specific part of the brain. Of course, we all know worrying is charged with more negative emotions. Worry keeps you from focusing on and putting energy into what's important in your life, can make it hard to connect with others, and is just flat-out mentally exhausting.

Anxiety is physically based, showing up as bodily symptoms, actions, and behaviors, and primarily involves your limbic system interacting with parts of the brain to turn on your fear circuit. Oftentimes, anxiety doesn't have a conscious component that you can readily point to as the cause and will simply pop up as a symptom, like an upset stomach, headache, or shortness of breath.

According to The Anxiety And Depression Association Of America, anxiety disorders have become the most common mental diagnosis in the U.S., cost the country $42 billion in 1999, and go hand-in-hand with depression. People with an anxiety disorder are three to five times more likely to go to the doctor and six times more likely to be hospitalized for a psychiatric illness.

Put simply, worrying is *thinking* about something, and anxiety is *feeling* it.

Worry and anxiety are not all bad and developed for your protection. Both are really your brain's way of learning from past experiences to try to steer you clear of potential dangerous situations in the future. Your brain's number one priority is keeping you alive, and it's evolved to this very well. When something bad happens, your thinking brain notes everything that preceded the event and tries to figure out patterns and connections within that occurrence and to past bad experiences that might have predicted it.

When remembering a deadly predator's territory meant the difference between life or death, these traits were evolutionary advantages which greatly aided our species in thriving. But today when your brain can find a hundreds of reasons every day to sound the alarm and connects things that don't have any correlation, these circuits activate too frequently and can get stuck in the on position causing serious negative results for your mental and physical health. In his book, *The Upward Spiral: Using Neuroscience to Reverse the Course of Depression, One Small Change at a Time*, Alex Korb describes it like this:

> *Imagine you're a baseball pitcher and you have a hat you always wear, and then one day you don't wear the hat, and you lose the game and feel ashamed. Your limbic system wants to avoid that feeling in the future, so it notices, 'Hey, I forgot to wear my hat. that must be the reason I lost.' Even though not wearing your lucky hat probably didn't cause the loss, once your limbic system assumes a possible connection, it becomes hard to unlearn it. From then on, not wearing the hat triggers anxiety.*[1]

While anxiety and fear activate the same stress response in your brain and body, triggering the release of hormones such as adrenaline and cortisol, they too are different. Fear is a reaction to *actual* danger, right here right now. Anxiety is concern over *potential* danger -- unpredictable events which you probably don't have control over.

Worry is in your mind. So, to reduce it, you have to learn to soothe and guide your thinking brain and calm its fear circuit. Some ways to do that are:

1.   Become aware of your emotions.

To decrease worry, you have to first recognize when you're doing it. Becoming aware of your emotional state as it occurs (mindfulness - which we'll talk more about later) enlists your thinking frontal cortex and suppresses the fight or flight amygdala response. In one study, when participants simply labeled an emotion, their brains settled down.

2.   Practice conscious breathing.

Taking slow, deep breaths through your nose into your diaphragm with slow exhales turns down your nervous system reducing your body's stress response. Slow, deep breathing stimulates the calming parasympathetic nervous system and sends your body and mind the message "I'm relaxed."

3.   Stay in the present.

When you find your mind drifting to the past or future, come back to the right here and now. In this moment, you're OK. It's your thoughts creating the sense of danger. Bringing your awareness back into the now (also mindfulness) calms the brain's fearful amygdala and engages thinking neural circuits. (See chapter 16)

4.   Focus on what you can control.

Your brain craves control and feels happier and calmer when it perceives more control, even if it's just an illusion. Feeling more in control has been shown to reduce anxiety, worry, and even physical pain. Avoid imagining the worst possible scenarios, and pay more attention to what is in your control, which modulates brain activity to reduce anxiety. (BTW - Research shows that around 85% of the time things turned out better than people feared, and they handled them way better than they thought they would.)

5.   Make a decision - any decision.

Simply making a decision about whatever it is that you're worrying invokes your thinking brain, increases your dopamine levels, and shifts your brain's perceptual focus to the things that matter the most. Making a decision also elevates your perceived control giving your confidence and mood a boost which helps propel you to act positively. Studies show that negative thinking and anxiety both decrease with decisiveness.

6.   Go for good enough.

Worrying is often triggered by imposing unrealistic or perfectionist expectations on yourself or others. Don't aim for being the best at work. Just meet your goals. Your partner doesn't have to do everything right. They just need to care about you and put honest effort into the relationship. You don't have to have abs of steel. You just want to be healthy. If you cut yourself and others some slack, you'll be happier.

Anxiety is in your body and can be understood by remembering "The ABC's of Anxiety" according to Alex Korb which is also key to taming it.

Alarm - You observe something that your brain thinks is worthy of sounding the alarm. Just like worry, the first step in decreasing anxiety is to become aware of it. Notice that your heart is racing or that your breathing has become shallow in the moment as it is happening. Consciously try to determine a causal link to an event or situation, past, present, or future, before your brain rushes on to the next step.

Belief - You evaluate the alarm and make a belief about it. Beliefs are most often subconscious and based on past programming, wounds, and experiences. Here's your chance to interrupt the downward spiral of anxiety before it spins out of control by recognizing automatic negative thinking patterns, like catastrophizing, black and white thinking, and assuming, and consciously working with your mind to reframe thoughts and insert new beliefs that empower and encourage you.

Coping - You respond to the belief. Coping can be a subconscious, non-productive habit, like eating a pint of Ben and Jerry's or having a Netflix marathon or productive, conscious response, like going for a walk or taking a yoga class. It's entirely possible to change coping skills from negative bad habits to healthier, more positive routines which will help to decrease the problem of anxiety in the first place. What really has to happen is you have to change the habits in your brain.

Chapter Eleven

The Toxic Cycle Of Stress

The greatest weapon against stress is our ability to choose one thought over another.

William James

To experience absolutely no stress, you would have to be dead.

Seriously.

Stress is your body's natural and necessary physical reaction to changes in its environment or circumstances where your brain perceives a response is necessary for your protection.

When stressed, your heart beats faster, your pupils dilate, your muscles tense, your breathing increases, more blood is pumped to your muscles, and adrenaline and other hormones are secreted into the bloodstream to prepare you to fight for your life or flee. Your breathing increases to oxygenate all that extra blood. Back when our caveman ancestors were predators and prey, stress was absolutely essential for survival.

Not all stress is bad. Even though you probably don't have to run for your life often these days, stress can still be a positive thing, called eustress, providing motivation, energy, and focus, helping you perform at your best, and even increasing productivity. The jitters a person feels before making a presentation (extreme nausea in my case), the drive to achieve a goal, or the thrill of a roller coaster ride (nausea again) would be examples of eustress.

Many things in life, such as planning a wedding, working in a challenging job, or even moving to a bigger house are considered good things yet still come with lots of stress. Eustress actually helps keep you happy, healthy, and gives life meaning. Without it, life would be dull and flat, but even too much eustress can tax your system.

Stress is a normal bodily response and isn't good nor bad by itself. When your body has a stress reaction to every little thing that happens: a snide comment by your partner, running late for a meeting, or the growing credit card bill, then there's a problem. When stress becomes an almost constant state and chronic condition, it has negative, lasting consequences for your mind and body.

Back when most humans died around middle age, the benefits of the bodily stress activation outweighed the long-term costs. but today, with people living much longer, the cumulative damage of chronically over stimulating this system leads to gastrointestinal, immune, cardiovascular, and endocrine problems with the greatest impact usually being seen on a person's psychological well-being as increased anxiety and depressed mood.

The key word here is chronic.

Chronic stress sets up a vicious cycle in which stress is usually a precursor to anxiety, and anxiety is usually a precursor to depression. If you are under stress and don't find ways to release the stress after the event has passed or learn techniques to cope during, you carry around a constant current of worry that can become ingrained as anxiety. And then if you suffer from anxiety for too long, chances are that you could slip into depression. This sets up a vicious cycle that is hard to break out of.

In the *10 Reasons Why Stress Is The Most Dangerous Toxin In Your Life*, Dr. Robin Berzin states that:

> *Stress is possibly the most dangerous toxin your body faces every day because it changes your gene expression, causes brain damage, shuts down your immune system, increases inflammation, causes belly fat, and more.*[1]

Stressors can be real or perceived and sometimes you can't do much about real threats. It doesn't really matter which because when you think of something stressful, it creates the same stress response in your body. Real or imagined, the solution is to learn to manage, release, and de-escalate stress before it snowballs into anxiety and depression.

Fortunately, there are plenty of techniques and tools that can help you effectively manage and decrease stress. Some are:

1. **Address possible biological causes of stress**

Clean up your diet by eating more fruits and vegetables - preferably organic, reduce processed foods, artificial sweeteners, additives, and coloring. Eliminate the ingestion of toxins and exposure to them in your environments.

2. **Take a breather**

That may mean taking a deep breath and counting to five in a stressful moment or taking a walk at lunch during a busy day at work, or finding a hobby or activity that actively relaxes you.

3. **Come into the present moment**

Bring your mind to the right here and now. Become aware of your thoughts and reframe them to decrease anxiety. Scan your body for tension and consciously relax tense areas. (See chapter 16)

4. **Mediate**

If you don't already have a practice, start one. Research shows that daily meditation alters the brain's neural pathways making you more resilient to stress, strengthens your immune system, and increases serotonin, the happy neurochemical, production. (See chapter 22)

5. **Visualize**

Use your mind to calm your body by imaging yourself in any setting in which you feel calm and relaxed. Visualize your body and mind letting go of tension. You can also use guided imagery exercises to help you. (See chapter 23)

6. Connect with others

Lean on your social network. Talk to friends, and share what's going on. You can get a fresh perspective, support, and tactical help.

7. Melt the stress away

Get a professional massage or use a tennis ball or foam roller to massage away tension. Take a bath using essential oils for aromatherapy relaxation.

8. Laugh out loud

A good belly laugh doesn't just lighten the load mentally. It lowers cortisol, the stress hormone, and boosts brain chemicals, endorphins, which brighten your mood. Watch your favorite comedy, read a funny book, or spend time with someone who makes you laugh.

9. Crank up the tunes

Research shows that listening to soothing music can lower blood pressure, heart rate, and anxiety. You can create a soothing playlist or blow off steam by rocking out to more upbeat tunes.

10. Get moving

All forms of exercise, including yoga and walking, can ease depression and anxiety by helping the brain release feel-good chemicals and by giving your body a chance to release stress. Even everyday activities such as housecleaning or yard work can reduce stress. (See chapter 26)

11. Sleep more

Lack of sleep increases stress hormones. Get your eight hours no matter what and take a nap if you missed sleep. Prioritize it.

Chapter Twelve

Breaking Bad Habits In Your Brain

We become what we repeatedly do.

Sean Covey

Habits are those things you routinely do when you're not really paying attention and might seem to have very little to do with your brain. But it's because habits are etched into your brain that you don't have to actively think about them – which is also why they are so very hard to change.

What really has to happen is you have to change your brain.

Most of your daily actions are impulses or routines guided by your unconscious mind or in another word, habits. Habits are neuronal connections and paths created in your brain by repetition and there's a clear neuroscientific explanation for how they're formed, maintained, and changed.

Intentional actions are handled by your thinking brain, the prefrontal cortex. Habits are governed by the striatum, an ancient processing center located deep in your brain. In his book, *The Upward Spiral: Using Neuroscience to Reverse the Course of Depression, One Small Change at a Time*, Alex Korb, describes it this way: "If your prefrontal cortex is modern, cloud-based computing, then your striatum is punch cards fed into an IBM mainframe."[1]

Your striatum isn't even conscious and is perfectly happy carrying out bad habit after bad habit with no desire to change. But the little bugger, along with other areas, lets you tie your shoe or ride a bike without having to think about it every time. Of course, your actions aren't all unconscious and are coordinated by your nucleus accumbens, striatum, and prefrontal cortex.

Your nucleus accumbens is motivated by what you find pleasurable, and your striatum chooses what to do based on what's been done before. The only part that gives a hoot about your well-being is your prefrontal cortex, and it often gets outvoted.

Your nucleus accumbens craves the dopamine squirt that it knows goes with what it has learned to be pleasurable. The confounding thing is that the first time you do something; the dopamine comes after the action. In the future, the dopamine is released earlier and earlier until just thinking about something in anticipation causes a dopamine reward. So, the dopamine released before the action and along the way actually motivates you towards the behavior, and a bad habit is born.

Every time you follow the same path, a specific pattern is activated and becomes more defined in your striatum (the neurons that fire together become wired together) and it becomes easier to activate the circuit the next time and so on. Pretty soon, the bad habit neuronal pathway becomes the unconscious default, and your brain, wanting to be efficient, just takes the easiest, most familiar route.

This is particularly true in the case of depression. In a depressed brain, there's less dopamine activity happening in the nucleus accumbens which means things that used to be enjoyable are not as pleasurable, and the only things that motivate it have to have a big dopamine payoff, which are the baddest of the bad habits: junk food, risky behavior, drugs, alcohol, gambling, porn.

Interestingly, all bad habits aren't created equally. The ones which release the most dopamine require less repetition to form. For example, smoking causes a big hit of dopamine, and it doesn't take many cigarettes to pick up the practice. On the other hand, flossing your teeth doesn't give you a big dopamine surge unfortunately. When a person is stressed, they turn to coping habits which can either be good or bad. And in fact, stress biases your brain towards old habits over new actions.

How unfair is that?

Your oldest bad habits are probably the ones that you developed to cope and distract yourself as a child and are some of the deepest, most ingrained routines you have – and the hardest to break. But it can be done.

To break a destructive coping habit, very rarely can you just stop doing it cold turkey because you're still left with the original stress in your brain and body. You have to replace the undesirable habit with another, more positive one and take measures to reduce the stress that triggers unwanted habits in the first place.

When it comes to breaking bad habits – and in life in general, you'll have much more success by making your brain your friend instead of your enemy. You can stop the bad habit spiral by building more positive habits in your brain. When first trying to insert a new habit, it's going to require conscious effort, intention, and thought until you've done it enough for the connections to be made and strengthened in your striatum.

This means that in the beginning, your prefrontal cortex has to use conscious will to override the old patterns until the burden of action shifts to become the unconscious default of your striatum. You've might have heard that it takes 21 days to form a new habit. Unfortunately, this is not true, and there's no one size fits all answer here. The amount of time required to instill a new habit depends on what you're trying to do and can range anywhere from 3 weeks to many months or longer with there being a curved relationship between habit and automaticity.

In the article, "How Long It Takes to Form a New Habit," Maria Popova explains:

> It's like trying to run up a hill that starts out steep and gradually levels off. At the start you're making great progress upwards, but the closer you get to the peak, the smaller the gains in altitude with each step[2].

In the book, *The Upward Spiral: Using Neuroscience to Reverse the Course of Depression, One Small Change at a Time*, Alex Korb has the following suggestions for developing positive habits:

1. **Figure Out Your Triggers**

Determine what's going to cause the anticipatory dopamine squirt to motivate you towards a bad habit and avoid it. If possible, remove the trigger for any bad habit from your life, which could mean changing your environment subtly or drastically. It's much easier to avoid temptation than to resist it.

2.   Use Self-Affirmations

Studies show undeniably that using positive self-reflection helps significantly in establishing new habits. The self-encouragement doesn't have to be just about the desired behavior, an overall supportive attitude helps.

3.   Reduce Stress

If you don't perform the bad habits or coping mechanisms you always have, you stay stressed and get even more stressed because you can't release it in your typical way. Then, that stress motivates you further towards the undesired behavior in a vicious cycle. Ugh! You have to reduce your stress levels through practices such as exercise, meditation, mindfulness, gratitude, sleep, and social interaction. (See chapter 11)

4.   Accept That You Won't Be Perfect

In order to adopt better habits, you don't have to make zero mistakes. In fact, you will do better if you expect them as part of the process. You'll experience more success in your transformation if you enlist your prefrontal cortex by actively paying attention. Your brain has limited resources. When you stop paying attention because of distraction or stress, your brain shifts to the old default striatum patterns, and you end up eating a pint of ice cream. Every time you push forward with your goal, you're making the old habit weaker in your brain.

5.   Resolve To Change

Making a personal resolution to change has proven much more effective than simply wanting to change and increases your chances of success. Be specific and make action oriented decisions. For example, "I want to get more exercise" is not as effective as "I resolve to walk for an hour after work 3x a week."

6.   Increase Your Serotonin

Increasing serotonin activity helps your prefrontal cortex function properly and assert itself to override the bad habit striatum. There are many ways to increase serotonin naturally including get more sunlight, get a massage, exercise, and recall happy memories.

7.   Enlist Your Thinking Brain

Help your prefrontal cortex control your striatum by cultivating self-awareness. Keep long-term goals in mind; write them down; post them around your environment. Consciously think about how your life would improve by changing your habits. Remind and motivate yourself with affirmations, visualization, and celebrate small accomplishments.

8.   Practice Productive Procrastination

Instead of judging yourself harshly and stressing out when you don't feel like going to the gym, give yourself permission to defer an activity one time and make a non-negotiable appointment with yourself for later. Then, keep it. Once you get productive, your brain releases dopamine, and you'll have more energy and motivation to continue.

The first essential step to accomplishing change to improve your life is a simple awareness of your thoughts and behaviors. The second essential ingredient is believing that it can be done and making the choice to do it, which leads us to the next chapter.

Chapter Thirteen

Deciding Against Depression

Deciding what not to do is as important as deciding what to do.

Steve Jobs

When you're in the fog of depression, all too often you aren't able to make even small, everyday decisions - much less big ones - because you feel paralyzed and every option just seems wrong. In fact, indecisiveness is one of the things that makes depression so persistent and is part of a self-perpetuating downward spiral. A depressed person can't make definitive decisions to move forward, and they don't take positive action which only leads to more depression.

Making a decision - any decision - can help you to start to climb out of depression.

Think of it this way. You're supposed to have dinner with friends in a neighboring city, but one you don't know your way around in very well. The festivities start at 7:00 and it's 6:55. You're terribly lost and your cell phone is dead, which has the address and is your GPS. You remember putting the charger on the counter so you wouldn't forget it. But of course, you did.

If you continue driving around without a clue and never make a decision to ask for help, it's pretty certain that you'll never find your friends and have the wine and witty conversations you were looking forward to. On the other hand, if you decide to stop at a convenience store, ask to use a phone, look up the friend's number, call them, and get directions, you put the odds back in your favor. If you're stuck in a bad situation, you have to pick a direction and move forward because if you sit there and do nothing, you're screwed. Same with depression.

Often, there's not one clear right direction in which to go, and if you're depressed, you're likely to focus on all of the drawbacks of each option, not feeling really good about any of them. In this case, just making a good decision - not THE BEST decision - is better than doing nothing at all.

It doesn't do any good to put a bunch of stress on yourself to make *the right* decision and only contributes to the fearful stuck feeling that causes no decision to be made in the first place. Just make a decision that seems good at that time, move forward, and look around and decide where to go from there, which may mean switching paths altogether or not. Some movement is better than no movement.

Now, I'm not suggesting that you can just decide not to be depressed and magically get better. I'm saying that making a decision can be the beginning of a positive chain reaction in a depressed brain, helping it to build positive momentum in several ways.

In *The Upward Spiral: Using Neuroscience to Reverse the Course of Depression, One Small Change at a Time*, Alex Korb explains how this happens:

Deciding enlists your thinking brain and increases dopamine.

A depressed brain is stuck in habitual brain circuits loops that don't help the person get any better. Deciding engages the prefrontal cortex and helps it to override unconscious habit loops. The more you use particular brain pathways, the stronger they get, and deciding beefs up the part of the brain that lets you modulate habits and impulses and work towards goals.

Your prefrontal cortex is responsible for goal-directed behavior which means it controls which goals you pursue and how you get there. The first step in successfully achieving goals is making decisions. Once a decision is made, your brain releases dopamine to keep you motivated with every step and achievement along the way. Research shows that reaching the final goal is often less important to happiness than setting the goal in the first place.

Deciding focuses attention and enhances perception.

When you make a decision, your prefrontal cortex helps you filter out irrelevant distractions and focus on your goal. Making a decision actually alters your brain's perception to guide you to pay attention to the things that matter the most. Your prefrontal cortex has top-down control over your senses and can actually tell your vision and hearing what to ignore helping it not get overwhelmed. Making a decision changes your brain's perceptual processing of the world.

Korb describes it this way:

> *Of course, changing the way your brain perceives the world is not going to solve all your problems. Imagine you're trying to find your car keys in the dark. Turning on the light will not magically reveal them — maybe they're in the pants you were wearing yesterday or under the couch cushions. But turning on the light will sure as heck improve your chances of finding them. Making a decision, even a tiny decision, starts shedding light on ways to improve your life.* [1]

Deciding creates perceived control.

Your brain craves certainty and control and indecisiveness contributes to an unhappy brain. Lack of control causes stress and in the real world, you often don't have control over much. Interestingly, studies show that you don't even need control over what's causing you stress. As long as you have control over something, you get brain benefits.

The important thing here is not ultimate control (does that even exist?), but perceived control. Making decisions increases your perceived control giving your confidence and mood a boost which helps you to make more decisions and take positive action.

Deciding reduces worry and anxiety and increases enjoyment.

A decision is simply creating an intention to move forward in a particular direction which reduces the number of variables your thinking brain, the prefrontal cortex, needs to consider and optimize. Having too many choices can overwhelm the brain causing cognitive overload leaving a person mentally drained and stressed.

Studies show that negative thinking and anxiety both decrease with decisiveness. A person will actually benefit by narrowing their choices and focus to help with decision making. In fact, some studies have shown that having to make too many decisions can leave people tired, mentally drained and more dissatisfied with their decisions.

You might believe that you are happy when good things happen, but research indicates that people are happiest when they decide to pursue a particular goal, then achieve it.

Deciding helps you make more decisions in the future.

Every time you make a decision, you are strengthening the decision making circuit in your brain starting a positive cycle making it easier to activate in the future. Similarly, every time you worry, act impulsively, or procrastinate, you are strengthening those capabilities in your brain. Like a muscle, you have to build up your decision making brain circuits. Start by making small decisions about seemingly insignificant things. Research shows that being decisive in one area of your life can improve decisiveness in other parts of your life putting your brain in an upward spiral.

Pulling yourself out of depression is, of course, not as easy as just deciding to not be depressed anymore. However, making one tiny decision can be the catalyst for taking a small step forward which can build momentum to take another positive step, and so on. Before you know it, you've made some serious progress.

Chapter Fourteen

Responding vs. Reacting

When you react, you are giving away your power. When you respond, you are staying in control of yourself.

Bob Proctor

Again the distinction between the two words may seem to be insignificant, but the difference in your life can be huge. Reacting is an instinctual behavior directed by your brain being triggered by emotions, and responding is a conscious choice involving input from your more evolved brain.

In his book, *Just One Thing: Developing a Buddha Brain One Simple Practice at a Time*, Rick Hanson explains how the two differ in your brain. To simplify drastically, the human brain evolved in stages beginning with the reptilian brain, the brainstem, which is primarily concerned with avoiding harm. Next, the mammalian brain, the limbic system, developed which focuses on approaching rewards. Finally, the human brain, the cortex, formed which is all about attachment. In every human today, these three systems are constantly at work.

When anything happens in your environment to cause you feel the slightest bit threatened, which can range from someone cutting you off in traffic to a co-worker making a snarky remark, your reptilian brain activates in fight or flight reactive mode. A million years ago, this was a good thing to keep our ancestors alive; however, in today's world, it happens all too often.

Whenever you're pressured, worried, irritated, or disappointed this mechanism kicks in, which not only feels crummy and can lead to anxiety and depression, but is lousy for your long-term physical health. Chronic stress contributes to a weakened immune system and increased risk of heart attack and stroke.

In reactive mode your avoiding brain expresses fear and anger. The approaching brain goes into scarcity mode which shows up as greed ranging from longing to addiction. At the same time, your attachment system moves into hurt mode which can leave you feeling abandoned, worthless, or lonely. Not fun.

On the other hand, when you feel safe and fulfilled, your brain's avoidance system is calm, the approaching drive is content, and the attachment orientation is caring and receptive. In this responsive mode, your brain is soothed, joyful, and replenished. This is the natural, resting state of your brain and where you want to be for happiness and health; however too many of us spend most of our time in reactive mode.

Just as with emotions and feeling, reacting is instinctual; responding is a conscious choice. When something happens, your body is going to emote and react automatically regardless. The trick is to become aware of the initial emotions/reaction, resist doing anything, invoke your higher intelligence, considering options, possible ramifications, who you want to be, and what's going to be in your best interest, and then choose how you respond.

In the article, "Responding vs. Reacting," J. Loeks writes:

> *The act of responding requires one to look at the circumstance, identify the problem or situation, hear what is happening and reflect. That reflection can be for a moment, five seconds, one hour, two days or longer. The time frame doesn't matter. What matters is that you stopped and put an effort to think and suspended judgment. It is a conscious act and shows that you are willing to listen or observe. This 'gap' between the circumstance and your behavior is what contributes to gaining a sense of control in your life. Once a person can identify that in responding they actually have a choice in the manner, he/she will start to realize that they are able to make better decisions. The key is that pause. If the situation requires an immediate action, then just take a deep breath first. This alone can help one gain a semblance of control and make one choose an alternative statement or action that can make a big difference in an outcome of a situation.[1]*

Learning to respond rather than react took years, but made a huge positive difference in my life. I used to be an incredibly reactive drama queen which could make a bad situation or even a good situation worse really quickly and lead to damaging consequences. Take for example, trying to commit suicide resulting in a serious brain injury and losing custody of my sons.

I remember reading somewhere that the difference between responding and reacting was about ten seconds. For me, it can be much longer and, even then, I still don't get it right sometimes. It's amazing to me that I can sit on something for days, being good and not reacting, meditating on the issue and consciously thinking about how I want to respond, only to fire off an email that I have convinced myself is non-reactive which I immediately realize is after hitting send.

I've adopted Joyce Meyer's quote as my personal motto: "You may have been given a cactus, but you don't have to sit on it." OK, over the years life gave me a whole cactus garden, but I was the one who kept plopping my butt on it. Every time I wallowed in self-pity; every time I tortured myself with painful memories; every time I knee-jerk reacted, I was taking a running jump and landing squarely on the thorns. I was only hurting myself. Admittedly, life wasn't great, but I was making an even bigger mess of it by my reactions.

I've learned that my experience of anything is determined not by the actual circumstances, but by my behavior and thoughts while going through the situation. Most of the pain and anguish I feel is caused by my struggle against "what is."

Pema Chodron, an American Buddhist nun, advises us to "lean into" painful situations and see what they have to teach us. In her book *The Wisdom of No Escape and the Path of Loving Kindness,* she writes:

> There's a common misunderstanding among all the human beings who have ever been born on the earth that the best way to live is to try to avoid pain and just try to get comfortable. You can see this even in insects and animals and birds. All of us are the same.
>
> A much more interesting, kind, adventurous, and joyful approach to life is to begin to develop our curiosity, not caring whether the object of our inquisitiveness is bitter or sweet. To lead a life that goes beyond pettiness and prejudice and always wanting to make sure that everything

*turns out on our own terms, to lead a more passionate, full,
and delightful life than that, we must realize that we can
endure a lot of pain and pleasure for the sake of finding out
who we are and what this world is, how we tick and how our
world ticks, how the whole thing just is.*[2]

When faced with tough times, I've developed a plan that
helps me to respond rather than react (I was trying to come up with a
catchy acronym, but couldn't. So it's AZFD! How's that?):

1. **Accept What's Before You**

Stop fighting the circumstances, people, or yourself. Quit
judging and shoulding yourself or others. It is what it is, and
you feel what you feel. There's nothing inherently good or
bad or right or wrong about any of it as these qualities exist
in your thoughts about what happens - not what's actually
happening. And you can drive yourself crazy shoulding all
over the place.

2. **Zoom Out**

Drop the story lines and your personal emotional
investment in the situation. Who did or said what doesn't
really matter in the end and won't help you get through it.
These details fuel your anger, hurt, and sense of injustice.
Broaden your perspective, take on different points of view,
and try to be objective.

3. **Focus on Yourself**

In any situation, the only thing you ever have control
over is yourself. Instead of looking for external sources and
pointing your finger there, turn the finger back around to you.
Take an honest look at your contribution to the situation and
your behavior. Ask yourself what you could do differently
going forward and what are the possible lessons or good
things that could come from this. To get different results, you
have to do something different. Not them. You.

4. Decide

Consciously decide who you want to be, how you want to behave, and what's going to be in your best interest. Hold that image in the forefront of your mind and move forward taking appropriate actions. Deciding is not a one-time thing. The priorities upon which you decide have to be considered and honored in the little choices you make every day.

I've had tremendous success using the above process. Now, that doesn't mean things have gone the way I wanted them to go every time or that I haven't lashed out. It means that I've been able to come back to or remain calm, eventually find some peace, and learn while moving through challenging experiences. Until I accept what's happening, I'm only causing myself pain and using my energy to struggle against what's before me instead of working with it for my highest good.

When I consciously direct my thoughts and behavior to respond, the situation can then unfold on its own schedule and work itself out. My job is to control myself and make sure that I don't fling myself on a cactus.

Learning to become non-reactive is a continual challenge, an everyday thing, but it does get easier the more you override the reptilian brain engaging your responsive brain. Rick Hanson writes in *Just One Thing: Developing a Buddha Brain One Simple Practice at a Time*:

> *Each time you rest in your brain's responsive mode, it gets easier to come home to it again. That's because "neurons that fire together, wire together": stimulating the neural substrates of calm, contentment, and caring strengthens them. This also makes it harder to be driven from home; it's like lengthening the keel of your mental sailboat so that no matter how hard the winds of life blow, you stay upright, not capsized, and keep on heading towards the lighthouse of your dreams.[3]*

The responsive mode of your brain can be activated, encouraged, and reinforced through mindfulness practices, meditation, and coming into the present moment, all of which are free and available to everyone all the time. Think of situations in your own life where you would benefit from responding rather than reacting. Bet you can come up with a few.

Chapter Fifteen

The Meaning Of Mindfulness

The awareness that emerges through paying attention on purpose, in the present moment, and nonjudgmentally to the unfolding of experience moment by moment.

Jon Kabat Zinn

Mindfulness has become one of those trendy terms that you see everywhere these days, but what exactly does it mean? Does it mean you have to burn incense, meditate like a monk, or quit eating meat? No.

To be mindful means simply to be aware. It's about remembering to be aware of your journey through life as it's happening, even the little things or especially the little things. Mindfulness means staying out of your head in the present moment and not dwelling on the past or projecting into the future. Mindfulness means to become more conscious of what's going on around and within you.

To continue with the Triangle of Well-Being example from Chapter Five originating from Dr. Dan Siegel's book, *The Mindful Brain: Reflection and Attunement in the Cultivation of Well-Being*, he explains mindfulness as:

> *Mindfulness in its most general sense is about waking up from a life on automatic, and being sensitive to novelty in our everyday experiences. With mindful awareness the flow of energy and information that is our mind enters our conscious attention and we can both appreciate its contents and come to regulate its flow in a new way. Mindful awareness, as we will see, actually involves more than just simply being aware: it involves being aware of aspects of the mind itself. Instead of being on automatic and mindless, mindfulness helps us awaken, and by reflecting on the mind, we are enabled to make choices and thus change becomes possible.[1]*

As indicated above, being mindful is not only being aware, it's being aware of your awareness and approaching the present experience with a reflective attitude including the qualities of curiosity, openness, acceptance, and love which Siegel uses the acronym COAL to remember.

According to Siegel, there are five basic factors of mindfulness:

1. **nonreactivity to inner experience** - perceiving feelings and emotions without having to react to them;

2. **observing/noticing/attending to sensations, perceptions, thoughts, feelings** - not avoiding and remaining present with sensations and feelings even when they are unpleasant or painful;

3. **acting with awareness/not on automatic pilot**, concentration/nondistraction - not breaking or spilling things because of carelessness, not paying attention, or thinking of something else;

4. **describing/labeling feelings with words** - expressing beliefs, opinions, and expectations;

5. **nonjudgmental of experience** - not criticizing oneself for having irrational or inappropriate emotions.[2]

Almost every culture and religion have practices that encourage and help people to develop awareness of the present moment or mindfulness including meditation, prayer, yoga, tai chi and qigong. These practices share the common theme of consciously focusing awareness in a very specific way which is also a fundamental part of Buddhist, Christian, Hindu, Islamic, Jewish and Taoist teachings, but I'm not talking religion here. Mindfulness isn't associated with any one religious orientation nor does it conflict with any. I'm talking mental health.

Because you're more aware of and open to what's going on around you, mindfulness allows you to notice new opportunities and things to appreciate which you might have missed otherwise. Mindfulness makes you conscious of what's going on within you so you can maintain a healthy self-esteem and are less likely to self-sabotage or get in the way of your own success.

Studies have shown mindfulness to significantly improve a variety of conditions including borderline personality disorder, obsessive compulsive thinking, eating disorders, post traumatic stress, and anxiety. Mindfulness has also proven helpful in preventing relapse of chronic depression and substance abuse.

Mindfulness isn't limited to defined practice sessions. You'll get the most benefit out of working mindfulness into your daily life. You don't have to make drastic changes in order to be more mindful, you can begin in small ways:

1. Chew your food.

Sit down at a table and enjoy your meal. Slow down and be aware of sensations while you eat; turn off all gadgets and think consciously about what you're eating, how it got to your plate, and how it nourishes your body. Not only will this reduce the indigestion you might get from wolfing down a plate that you barely tasted, but it will also allow you to actually appreciate your meal mindfully.

2. Breathe deeply on purpose.

Almost all of us are guilty of shallow breathing, taking short rapid breaths that only expand the upper chest rather than engaging our diaphragms for deep belly breaths. Slowing down and becoming conscious of your breath not only lowers the heart rate, improves posture, and increases energy, but it calms your nervous system. Your breath is always with you and is simple way of being present and mindful anywhere.

3. Notice the good.

No matter what's going on in your life, there's always good to be found, even if it's something as small as turning the faucet and water coming out, the sun shining, or a bloom on your orchid plant. There was good in your past, there's good in the present, and there will be good in your future. You have to make a point to notice it.

4. Don't be afraid to say no.

Check in with yourself and say what you really mean making your happiness a priority. In every situation, there's always a caring way to respond considering what's being asked of you while factoring in your own needs and happiness. Stay aware when making decisions and conscious of the reasons behind those decisions - that's what being mindful is all about. Don't go through life operating from habit or avoidance. Take responsibility for your choices and be present while making them.

5. Get a hobby.

Meditation isn't confined to sitting on a cushion with your legs crossed and comes in all forms. Hobbies and activities that you enjoy can be among the best forms of meditation. When you become so engrossed in an activity, such a gardening, painting, yoga, running, being in nature, that you lose track of time and aren't thinking about your to-do list, you're doing light meditation. Getting lost in a hobby is an excellent way to be present and mindful. Or you can always begin a formal meditation practice.

After a while, being mindful becomes a way of life. It drastically changed my life and helped me recover from depression and the brain injury. It can change your life for the better too and help you to enjoy this crazy ride.

Chapter Sixteen

Right Here, Right Now

If you are depressed, you are living in the past.
If you are anxious, you are living in the future.
If you are at peace, you are living in the present.

Lao Tzu

To make sure that they didn't become a predator's next meal, our ancestors' brains developed a necessary vigilance and unease which continually scanned their outer and inner worlds for signs of danger. This tendency is still present in you today and is so automatic that you're probably not even aware of it, but it's always there showing up as anxiety, stress, and tension.

Neurologists estimate that a person is consciously aware of about 2,000 bits of information per minute. As impressive as that is, your brain is processing somewhere around 400 billion bits of information per minute, much of it below your conscious awareness. So, when you think you're not doing anything, your brain is actually still hard at work and is always on. This constant attentiveness can prevent relaxation and peace because your brain believes that you're never completely safe and can't let down its guard even for a minute. But, that's not true.

One way to turn your scanner down is to have your brain take a close look at *this* moment. Right here, right now, you're all right. Nothing is trying to eat you for dinner. No one is attacking you. You're not drowning. You're not dodging bullets. There's no immediate crisis. Everything in your life may not be perfect, but you're OK. Consciously realizing this is the act of coming into the present.

When you let your mind dwell in the future, called rumination, it creates worry and fear while delving into the past tends to conjure up regret and resentment. Indulging in these thought patterns too much can lead to depression.

Several times throughout your day, make a point of stopping what you're doing and noticing that you're all right, right now. The bills may be piling up with you having no idea of how they're going to get paid. Your mother may have Alzheimer's and taking care of that situation is wearing on you. You may be starting to wonder if there really is someone out there for you, *but* in this moment, your heart is beating, you're breathing, there's a roof over your head, and food in your belly. Underneath all of the circumstances, desires, and wants, you're OK. While fixing dinner, walking through the grocery store, driving to work, or reading emails, take the time to come into the present and reassure your brain, "I'm all right, right now."

In the book, *Just One Thing: Developing a Buddha Brain One Simple Practice at a Time*, Rick Hanson, writes:

> *Sometimes you're really not all right. Maybe something terrible has happened, or your body is very disturbed, or your mind is very upset. Do what you can at these times to ride out the storm. But as soon as possible, notice that the core of your being is okay, like the quiet place fifty feet underwater, beneath a hurricane howling above the sea.[1]*

Coming into the present moment calms your mind and soothes your sympathetic nervous system, reducing stress and anxiety in your brain and body. With dedicated practice, over time, your natural state can become relaxed and peaceful.

The simple, but powerful practice of realizing that "I'm all right, right now" has helped me to quit overreacting and get through many nerve-wracking situations without freaking out.

Chapter Seventeen

The Law Of Little Things

Enjoy the little things in life, for someday you will realize they were the big things.

Kurt Vonnegut

Some mental discomfort is inevitable in our lives because we evolved into feeling beings emotionally invested in others, and we experience distress when we think we or they are harmed, rejected, or hurt in some way. Running late for an important appointment, a weird look from your partner, or a worried thought about the credit card balance can be interpreted as a threat by your brain which sounds the alarm and causes your body to react accordingly.

Epinephrine gets your heart revved up so you can move fast. Norepinephrine sends blood to your large muscle groups and the bronchioles of your lungs while your pupils dilate to get ready to flee. Cortisol is pumped through your body suppressing your immune system to reduce inflammation from wounds. Your emotions intensify, and as limbic and endocrine activation increase, the executive functioning of your brain decreases.

In the harsh world of our evolving ancestors, this physical chain of reactions to serious threats helped our species survive. However, with the constant, low-grade stressors of our pedal-to-the-metal society today, this sometimes almost constant state of arousal creates unhealthy conditions for the mind and body with lasting consequences.

The cumulative damage of chronically overstimulating the fight-or-flight system over all these little things can lead to gastrointestinal, immune, cardiovascular, and endocrine problems with the greatest impact being seen on psychological well-being as anxiety and depression.

Most bodily systems and their responses are regulated by the autonomic nervous system (ANS) which operates mostly below your conscious awareness. The ANS has three wings: the sympathetic nervous system (SNS - fight or flight); the parasympathetic nervous system (PNS - rest and digest); and the enteric nervous system (regulates the gastrointestinal system).

The PNS and SNS evolved hand in hand to keep us alive. We need them both. However, if your SNS were surgically disconnected, you'd live. If your PNS were disconnected, you couldn't survive. Just like you can't drive a car by stomping on the gas and the brake at the same time, it's best for the SNS, the gas pedal, and the PNS, the brakes, to work together in balance.

In the book, *Buddha's Brain: The Practical Neuroscience of Happiness, Love, and Wisdom,* Rick Hanson suggests that you want to learn to exist predominantly in a baseline state of parasympathetic arousal with mild SNS activation for enthusiasm, vitality, wholesome passions, and occasional spikes to deal with demanding situations.

Of course, to do this takes practice, but you can learn to turn down your ANS and give more power to your PNS to create more peace and calm. Hanson writes:

> *The most powerful way to use your mind-body connection to improve your physical and mental health is through guiding your ANS. Every time you calm the ANS through stimulating the PNS you tilt your body toward inner peace and wellbeing.[1]*

Just as a lot of little stressors can add up to big problems, a lot of little moments of consciously calming your brain and body can make a big difference. Deliberately taking steps to make you feel safer turns down your ANS, helping control the hardwired tendency of your brain to look for and overreact to threats.

To relax your ANS:

1. mindfulness/ relaxation/visualization/affirmations,
2. connect with others,
3. become aware of fear itself,
4. come into the present,
5. be realistic,
6. increasing your sense of secure attachment in world.

To turn up your PNS:

1.   practice relaxing breathing exercises,
2.   exhale really big,
3.   touch your lips,
4.   be mindful of your body,
5.   consciously slow your heartbeat,
6.   meditate.

Finding refuge in whatever brings peace and calm and is a refueling station for you, whether it's people, activities, places, or something intangible such as a higher power or purpose, will increase the PNS calming response in your body and your overall feelings of happiness. With repetition and neuroplasticity, your brain becomes calmer and less reactive.

It's that simple to rewire your brain. Simple, but not easy.

Chapter Eighteen

Look For The Good And You'll Find It

If you look for the light, you can often find it. But if you look for the dark, that is all you will ever see.

Uncle Iroh from Avatar -The Last Airbender

The dishwasher overflowed last night, and you woke up to a kitchen floor full of suds. You found out two days ago that the mole on your Dad's ear was malignant. A monster typhoon slammed into the Philippines and left 10,000 dead.

Everywhere you turn these days there's more than enough stress, chaos, and bad news. It's easy to feel overwhelmed, anxious, and just flat-out disgusted with it all. How do you find good, happiness, and joy when there's so much bad?

You have look for it, notice it, and take it in. That's how.

As Rick Hanson explains in *Hardwiring Happiness: The New Brain Science of Contentment, Calm, and Confidence*, your brain doesn't automatically recognize the good stuff for two reasons. First, there isn't usually a stimulus to catch your attention in something good. There's no threat, no fear, nothing to make your brain take note. Remember, your brain's priority is your survival, and it looks for threats not rainbows. It doesn't automatically notice all the catastrophic things that *didn't* happen. Second, through a process called habituation, your brain filters out things that are routine and don't change, whether it's the refrigerator's hum or the absence of disasters in your daily life. So you become blind to the good that is there.

Although habituation is an efficient use of your neural resources, it causes a lot of the good that's around you to go unnoticed. To counteract this tendency of your brain, you have to intentionally look for, put emphasis on, and create good experiences. To do this, you have to become aware of the good present in your life and make those thoughts embodied experiences accompanied by good feelings, sensations, desires, and actions.

Hanson's not talking about making anything up here. He only asks that we see what's already there and shift our perspectives, which doesn't mean denying the less than desirable circumstances that exist. It means choosing to focus on and put energy into the things that could yield positive experiences for you.

Hanson writes:

> *Often we see a good fact but don't have any feelings about it. This seemingly small step – from idea to embodied experience – is critically important, for without it, there's not much to install in your brain. In terms of building neural structure, what matters is not the event or circumstance or condition itself but your **experience** of it.*[1]

So how, exactly, do you do this? You take in the good by noticing a positive that's already present or creating one. He suggests finding good facts in your current setting, recent events, ongoing conditions, personal qualities, the past, and the lives of others.

You're alive. You ate today. The sun is out. Your friend called a couple of days ago just to see how you were. You exercised yesterday. You're smart. You earned a college degree and nabbed that award at work last year. Your cousin just had a healthy baby boy. You get the idea. These small, but good things can be turned into embodied experiences by tuning into your body and allowing yourself to really feel the positive emotions and sensations accompanying the thoughts. It's important to follow through on any positive actions that might occur to you with the events.

Good facts are all around you every moment of every day. Even bad things contain the seeds for good experiences. It might feel cheesy at first, but learn to look for the silver lining or at the very least, the lesson in every situation. Are you stronger for having had the experience? What did you learn?

You have to intentionally look for the good in the bad. Sometimes, it's darn near impossible to find good or create a good experience. You might be in excruciating pain, have suffered a traumatic loss, be buried in depression or caught in a panic. That's

OK. That's being human. Be gentle with and have compassion for yourself, accept where you are, ride out the storm, and look for the good when the time feels right.

After my suicide attempt, I was seriously brain injured and had lost custody of my two sons who moved to a different state with their father. In the years that followed, I *had* to consciously look for the good around me because there wasn't much readily apparent anymore, and it did feel forced and fake at first. But it still felt a heck of a lot better than focusing on all that was wrong.

At times, I had to get out the magnifying glass, but good was always still there if I looked hard enough. I just had to notice it. The sun warming my cheeks as I walked the dog on a chilly morning; the silkiness of the cat's fur as I scratched her rumbling chin with her curled up on my lap; a really good tune playing on my iPod were the smallest of joys, but joys nonetheless.

Noticing the good has become an essential element in my mental health tool box. It's a choice, costs nothing, and anyone can do it anywhere anytime. With practice, making a conscious effort to notice the good and internalizing it becomes a habit which makes it easier to maintain a positive state of mind even when chaos is swirling around you.

While you're establishing a practice of looking for the good, it will help if you also limit the bad. Television programs and news shows, newspapers, and electronic media highlight and sensationalize the drama, the horrible, and the attention-getting shockers. Now, I'm not telling you to stick your head in the sand.

There's no way to avoid all media, and you don't want to, but there's also no need to focus on the negative hype and let it scare and worry you to death. Find sources that report the good (they do exist), inspire, and motivate you instead.

Over time because of neuroplasticity, the practice of looking for the good actually changes the neuronal structure of your brain hardwiring it for happiness. Look for the good, and you'll find it. Promise.

Chapter Nineteen

Making Fear Your Friend

Everything you want is on the other side of fear.

Jack Canfield

I've lived most of my life according to the "shoulds," doing all the things that I was told were right to achieve the good life I'd heard about growing up. To get to this promised land, I invested most of my efforts into trying to avoid the big, scary, bad things I'd learned that I didn't want: pain, loneliness, and failure.

With fear looming large in the background, the major decisions in my life were all about what I didn't want instead of what I did want. Life became an obstacle course of avoiding rather than achieving, which led to a numb, depressed existence, culminating in the suicide attempt. If medals were handed out for avoidance skills, I would've taken my place on the top podium.

Unhappy and stunted, I stayed in a marriage for far too long because I was terrified of going out on my own. After summoning the guts to leave, I dived headfirst into an unhealthy relationship primarily because I was afraid of being alone. Next, rather than face that break up and more legal entanglements with the ex, I tried to kill myself. Oh yeah, I was a real expert.

Surprisingly, avoidance can be an unconscious motivating factor behind much of our lives. Instead of having a clear idea of who we want to be, what we want, and making decisions accordingly which may involve some risk and discomfort, all too often, we make fear-based decisions, limiting us and our happiness. These choices may steer our actions and behavior in a direction allowing us to avoid some pain, but this path usually doesn't provide any real opportunity for substantial personal growth or even get us to our goals.

In your brain, avoid mode wins over approach mode every time because it could have meant the difference between life or death to our ancestors. This natural built-in tendency to choose safety over uncertainty doesn't do you much good today causing you to miss opportunities and live a smaller, anxiety-filled life. In one study, even a small amount of ambiguity caused increased activity in the brain's amygdala, deep brain structures involved in the processing and expression of emotions, especially fear. As the level of ambiguity and amygdala activity increases, the part of our brains involved in approaching rewards decreases functioning. Our brains don't merely prefer certainty over ambiguity, they crave it.

Your brain is programmed to seek certainty and the feeling of being right and in control, called "certainty bias," and when your brain feels like it has achieved this, it's happy. It doesn't matter if you actually are or not. In the book, *Nerve: Poise Under Pressure, Serenity Under Stress, and the Brave New Science of Fear and Cool,* Taylor Clark writes:

> *The more certainty and control we think we have about a potentially threatening situation, the less stress we will feel. Interestingly enough, perception is all that counts with this. You don't actually need to have perfect certainty or total control over how things will pan out; you just need to believe that you have them.*[1]

Our brains' innate desire for certainty in an increasingly uncertain world has caused anxiety to surpass depression in the past decade to become the most prevalent mental health issue in the United States. According to Clark, to calm our amygdala down and reduce stubbornness, fear, and anxiety we have to transform our relationship with fear from adversarial to accepting. Clark writes: "So, the measure of our ability to deal well with fear. isn't *whether* we get afraid, but how we *connect* with that fear."

Mother Nature was kind enough to program your amygdala with certain fears at birth, and you picked up many more from the world around you, the people in your life, and your experiences. When you get that anxious feeling, you need to ask yourself if it's really warranted or if it's just your brain's instinctual reaction to the unfamiliar and unknown. From your brain's perspective, to get over a fear, you have to expose yourself to it.

Because your brain is actually designed to thwart your conscious efforts to override the fear response, changing your relationship to fear isn't easy, but it can be done by becoming more mindful, getting comfortable with uncertainty, and even welcoming and leaning into fear.

Here are some tips to help you relate better to your fears and worries and reduce anxiety:

1. **Breathe**

   Consciously take slow, deep breaths into your abdomen to calm your ANS (autonomic nervous system) and tell your PNS (parasympathetic nervous system) that everything's OK.

2. **Put your feelings into words**

   Labeling fears and anxieties, through talking or writing, helps your brain process and diffuse them.

3. **Practice and be prepared**

   Through repetition and experience, you can train yourself to be more calm and make better decisions under stress because the situation becomes routine in the brain.

4. **Redirect your focus away from your fears**

   Instead of feeding and growing your fears, concentrate your attention on the present moment and task at hand.

5. **Mindfully detach from your worries and thoughts**

   Learn to non-judgmentally observe your thoughts and worries, distance yourself from them, and let them go without getting hooked into them.

6. **Expose yourself to your fears**

   To calm a fear, you have to allow yourself to actually be afraid and expose yourself to it.

7. **Learn to accept uncertainty and the fact that you aren't in control**

   By facing your fears, even exploring them, and accepting what is and your lack of control, you and your amygdala habituate to the circumstances and calm down. With exposure and acceptance, a fear loses its power.

8.   Reframe the situation

When anxiety does show up, consciously reframe your thoughts, look for the good and possible positive outcomes, and challenge negative thinking.

9.   Laugh about it

Research shows that humor helps a person break out of a negative point of view and see things with a brighter perspective.

10.   Build faith in yourself

Celebrate your small successes along the way when overcoming a fear, become aware of your internal voice and practice positive self-talk, and visualize optimistic outcomes to expand your comfort zone and confidence.

11.   Believe in a higher purpose

Dedication to something bigger than yourself, whether it's a spiritual belief, altruism, or personal goals, helps ease fear and keeps you going when the going gets tough.

12.   Open up to fear

Instead of fighting, avoiding, trying to control, or feeling bad about being afraid, learn to see fear as normal, expecting it to show up and exploring it when it does. If you stop thinking of fear as a problem, it's not a problem.

Being open to accepting, exploring, and making friends with your fears allows you to live a conscious life making decisions leading you closer to what you want instead of worrying about and running from the exploding land mines that you don't want.

It's much more enjoyable this way!

Chapter Twenty

Ditch The Shoulds

What screws us up most in life is the picture in our head of how it's supposed to be.

Anonymous

For decades, I was the best at conjuring up and living in the world of "should." I could tell you exactly what I, my life, and home should look like. And then when life didn't measure up to these shoulds, which was almost always, I would be disappointed and criticize myself mercilessly.

Through eighteen years of marriage and for several years of single motherhood after, I tried to live up to the image I had of the with-it woman who could keep her man happy, use a power drill, edge the yard, and whip up a mouth-watering dinner in a sparkling kitchen resembling something in a magazine while I looked effortlessly fabulous the whole time. Needless to say, I nor my life ever fit this description – not even close.

After my messy divorce and disastrous post marriage relationship, I labeled myself a miserable failure as a woman and mother. I was the furthest from the "shoulds" that I had ever been. "This isn't how it's supposed to be!" I whined. My answer to straying so far off of the should path was to try to commit suicide resulting in the brain injury and losing custody of my sons. And, I thought I was off the path before?

I came to understand that I had been causing my own suffering and torturing myself with expectations of what I thought should be. I've come to realize that there is no such thing as "should be." There's only what is. You can alleviate a lot of anxiety, pain, and suffering by getting rid of the shoulds and consciously being open to and accepting of whatever unfolds. Many philosophies teach, and I've found that emotional torment and suffering comes from our attachment to our thoughts about what happens, not what actually happens. Pain originates in the space between our thoughts and what is.

In *Loving What Is: Four Questions That Can Change Your Life*, Byron Katie explains:

> *A thought is harmless unless we believe it. It is not our thoughts, but the attachment to our thoughts, that causes suffering. Thoughts are like the breeze or the leaves on the trees or the raindrops falling. they appear like that and through inquiry we can make friends with them. Would you argue with a raindrop? Raindrops aren't personal and neither are thoughts.* [1]

Katie advises you to meet your thoughts with understanding and inquiry and proposes that behind every uncomfortable feeling, there's a thought that's not true for you. To change the stressful, uncomfortable feelings, you must understand the thoughts causing them rather than looking outside of yourself at circumstances or people.

After the reflexive "aack!" feeling, acceptance of what is closes the gap between expectations and reality, ending the pain for me, and only then, can I begin to figure out how to make the circumstances work best for me. If you consciously identify and eliminate expectations as much as possible and remain open to whatever unfolds, you are in a much better position to see and take advantage of opportunities that you might otherwise miss.

With a nonchalant shrug, an enlightened mind might think "Oh, now this" when something shows up because they were without expectations to begin with. While I'm not anywhere near that yet, I'm much closer than I used to be. I find it helpful to remind myself that just because events cause me pain or aren't what I expected or wanted, doesn't mean that whatever's happening isn't in my highest good or can't turn out OK or for the best even in the end.

So many times, circumstances which I pegged as undesirable at first, turned out to be just fine, when all was said and done. From experience, I've learned not to even begin to presume that I know what's best in any situation. What you like, want, and think you need isn't always going to provide growth or even get you to your goal, oftentimes. By trying to force a certain outcome, you limit other unforeseen possibilities which could be awesome and bring what you were seeking in the first place.

There really are no shoulds. Given that our individual brains uniquely interpret stimuli from our environments to create our individual realities, I have a hard time understanding how I or anyone can know what someone should believe or do or what is right for them. Shoulding someone or yourself or needing to be right indicates inflexible and limited thinking, assumes superiority, and judges another person or yourself. Needing to be right or to meet a "should" is usually a waste of your time and energy which could be put to better, more positive use in your life.

I once read a story that perfectly exemplifies this idea. Two deer were standing on railroad tracks arguing about the right direction in which to go. While they were arguing, a train ran over them.

Giving up expectations and the need to be right and keeping an open mind can lead to a happier, more peaceful life and provide new opportunities for growth and learning. A person not invested in being right can live life not being afraid to make mistakes and can laugh more easily at themselves when they inevitably do.

Life gets infinitely easier when you stay open without expectations, shoulds, or needing to be right.

Chapter Twenty-One

You Are Not Your Thoughts

Change your thoughts, and you change your world.

Norman Vincent Peale

The complex process of what's happening inside your head when your brain generates thought is not totally understood, but at the most basic level, your thoughts are nothing more than some electrical signals. As explained earlier, your experience of the world, your reality, is created by your thoughts, but you are not your thoughts or even accountable for the things that pop into your head. You can have an angry thought, but you are not angry. Your thoughts are. You are not sad. Your thoughts are. Be careful what labels you put on yourself.

The concept and understanding that I'm not my thoughts was huge for me. I didn't get this until my mid-forties after the suicide attempt, (I know. I was a little late.) and I used to believe I was a horrible person because of some of the things I would think. Now, I still have some shocking, wacky thoughts, but I don't define myself by them anymore, but rather I find them amusing. These days, I've learned to consciously choose which thoughts I believe and act on. It's a choice. You can't choose what you think, but you can always pick which thoughts you buy and put energy into.

Every spontaneous thought that comes into your head is influenced by that subconscious, internal chatter colored by your wounds and conditioning. At any moment, you have the power to observe the thought, argue with, and reframe it. Get an attitude even and say, "Hey, wait a minute! I don't buy that crap anymore and don't want to think that way. I'm going to choose to think like this." Thought reframing, consciously becoming aware of your thoughts and repositioning them, was a life-changer for me because it pulled me out of my depressive, negative thinking patterns.

Thought reframing can be practiced on-the-spot or as part of meditation, visualizing, or saying affirmations. With repetition, through neuroplasticity, this practice has been proven to physically alter brain circuits helping ease anxiety, depression, and OCD.

What I found so effective about thought reframing is that I didn't have to try to not have negative thoughts nor did I have to criticize myself for having them in the first place. Many cultural philosophies and religions are guilt-based, teaching us that a person is bad and should feel shame for having not-so-nice thoughts. Under no circumstances can you ever control what thoughts come into your brain. You don't even consciously generate these. Your mind does on auto mode.

Don't believe me? Try predicting what your next thought is going to be. If you controlled them, you would know, right? Attempting to control your thoughts and judging yourself harshly for not being able to do it is a self-defeating struggle. All you can ever take charge of is how you respond to the thoughts that do arise, and you don't have to judge yourself or your thoughts no matter how negative, inappropriate, or crazy they are.

In the space between observing your thoughts and choosing which ones to believe and act on is your chance to change your life because you can intentionally respond rather than react out of habit. Reacting is instinctual. Responding is conscious choice. When something happens, your body and brain are going to react automatically. Just like thoughts, you can't control this.

Through meditation and mindfulness, I've learned to detach from my thoughts, observe them, and choose the ones in which I invest and put energy. This feat has taken years, but has made a tremendous positive difference in my life, and it can do the same for you.

Chapter Twenty-Two

The Myth And Magic Of Meditation

The things that trouble our spirits are within us already. In meditation, we must face them, accept them and set them aside one by one.

Christopher L. Bennett

Yes, myth. Now don't get me wrong. I'm a huge fan of meditation. Meditation has been scientifically proven to strengthen the immune system, reduce blood pressure and the risk of stroke, minimize pain sensitivity, enhance cognitive function, and even grow a bigger brain. Meditation is the closest thing to a happy pill that I've found. However, there is one misnomer about meditation that I would like to clear up. Meditation isn't always peaceful.

When you see a picture of someone meditating they typically have that blissful, other-world expression on their face, and you can just see the peaceful vibes coming off of them like heat radiating off pavement on a hot summer day. It's this image that intimidates people so much that they don't even try to meditate or if they do start, they quickly end up frustrated, feeling as if they are failing miscrably.

The actuality of meditation, especially at first, may be nothing like that picture. In the beginning, meditation often isn't particularly peaceful, serene, or calm. Far from it. When first starting to meditate, you're going to wonder what in the heck you're trying to do and if you're doing it anywhere near right. Meditation may feel awkward, confusing, and uncomfortable at first, and bring up all sorts of emotions and issues from the past and present. Meditation can be emotional, upsetting, ugly – the exact opposite of peaceful.

When I first started meditating, I'd cry. And, I don't mean just a few, dainty tears. I mean whole body, shoulders-heaving, nose-running, can't-catch-your-breath, wailing sobs. I would also have anger surface so intense that I would scream and hit a pillow.

Now, that's not typically what you think of when you think of meditation, but I'm here to tell you that's part of it. This almost violent regurgitation of emotions is what a person may encounter when first beginning to meditate. Or you may not. What's right is whatever happens for you.

The purpose of meditation is to exercise a passive awareness of your mind objectively, become detached from your thoughts and feelings, and observe rather than identify with them. So, in meditation you just let the feelings come – the good, the bad, and the ugly – without labeling or judging them. I found this ridiculously difficult at first, as does most everyone, but, therein is the most beneficial work of meditation.

When beginning, all the scum, past wounds, old hurts, lingering grudges, and residual resentments are going to surface. It can be unpleasant, unsettling, scary, painful, and absolutely no fun. BUT it's good work that heals and helps you become a whole, healthy, happy person. That's the magic of meditation.

As layers of the crappy stuff are peeled back, you can start to sometimes achieve that goofy grin that goes with glimpses of peace and bliss. To get to this level can take years of practice and is not a steady state by any means. It's not as if you graduate from one level to the next permanently. When dealing with challenging or emotional issues, you're going dip back into the work mode of meditation, and it can get ugly again. That's the whole point, if you ask me.

Within reason, there really is no wrong way to meditate in my opinion, although there are plenty who will tell you differently. Trying to meditate is meditating, and any time spent with the awareness and intention to meditate is meditation as far as I'm concerned. When you give up any goals that you may have around the practice, such as quieting your mind, reaching enlightenment, or becoming one with the universe, you can actually start practicing meditation. When you give yourself permission to stop trying to halt your thoughts and just observe them impartially as they come, you eventually start to find the quiet space between your thoughts.

That's meditation. To put a bunch pressure on yourself to meditate "the right way" defeats the purpose. It's a learning process and can take years or a lifetime which is why it's called a practice.

Many schools of meditation make it way too complicated, but it doesn't have to be.

I like this quote by Osho:

> *You will have to understand one of the most fundamental things about meditation: that no technique leads to meditation. The old so-called techniques and the new scientific biofeedback techniques are the same as far as meditation is concerned. Meditation is not a byproduct of any technique.*[1]

Meditation also doesn't have to be spiritual or religious. It can simply be a mental health tool like breathing exercises or thought reframing because what you're really doing is training your mind and changing your brain. Research has shown that a healthy emotional style and mental habits can be cultivated and learned just like any other cognitive skill through meditation and mindfulness. Meditation will help you learn to respond mindfully instead of reacting mindlessly. Simply put, meditation makes you a happier person.

Meditation has been referred to as "Botox for the brain" because giving your brain a workout with meditation, just like you would exercise any other muscle, has been found to prevent cellular aging and the normal shrinkage of the brain that happens with age-related decline. People who meditate are less stressed, healthier, sleep better, and have a more positive outlook on life.

During meditation, the happy chemical, serotonin, is released and blood pressure decreases. Brain scans of meditators show higher activity in the frontal lobes which are essentially our humanness. There's also increased activity in the thalamus which aids different parts of the brain in talking to one another and is involved in the processing of sensory information.

Many studies have shown that participating in a meditation training program for as little as eight weeks can have measurable effects on the brain's amygdala, involved in processing fear anxiety and stress, even when someone isn't actively meditating. Meditation has also been shown to increase gray-matter density in the hippocampus, important for learning and memory, and in structures associated with self-awareness, compassion, and introspection. The practice builds a faster, fatter, and fitter frontal cortex, helping you to improve focus, concentration, and attention.

Meditation has even been shown to lengthen telomeres, the protective caps on the end of chromosomes, helping to slow the effect of the aging in the brain. Your telomeres are longest when you're young and naturally shorten as you age. Shorter telomeres have been associated with higher risk for many diseases including cancer.

I think doctors should prescribe meditation not medication. There are plenty of instructional guides on how to meditate out there. I learned from cds and books. So, I'll skip the in-depth how-to here, but I will give you the basics most everyone agrees on. There are many different flavors of meditation – some plain vanilla versions and some pretty far out there, but all practices usually involve three essentials: 1) Focus on something simple and non-thought-provoking like your breath, a single word, or sound. 2) Consciously relax your body. 3) Exercise a passive awareness of your mind.

That third element is the ridiculously hard part, but it's also the most beneficial. You've probably heard that in meditation you want to clear your mind of thoughts, but I want to tell you that that's a misconception. Maybe eventually, yes, but when learning, you don't have to try to clear your mind. Instead, let your thoughts, sensations, and whatever emotions you feel just flow without judgment and without getting wrapped up in them. If you do get hooked - and you most definitely will - label it "thinking," let it go, and return your awareness to your breath, sound, or word.

You already do light meditation even if you don't know it. This alpha brain state occurs when you become so engrossed in an activity that you lose track of time and aren't thinking about your to-do list. You're "in the zone" with your attention only on the task at hand while feeling a sense of calm. You may experience this while running, gardening, spending time in nature, writing, cooking, or whatever does it for you. I have a friend who says riding his motorcycle is meditative for him. This is the most relaxed a person can be and still be awake.

Deep meditation takes someone further into that half asleep, half-awake state where they're aware of their surroundings, but aren't actively conscious of them or interacting with the exception of moving meditations, like tai chi, yoga, and labyrinth walking. At this level of meditation, the brain produces theta waves which appear at the first stages of sleep.

Meditation doesn't have to be limited to sitting cross-legged on a cushion, you can do light meditation as described above and by being mindful in your daily activities. When you find yourself rushing around stressed out, take a few seconds to focus on your breath and become aware of and reframe any negative thoughts and feel your emotions When eating, really become aware of your food and the sensations you experience as you eat. At any moment, pay attention to your body's movements, how you're feeling, and what you're thinking.

I've been meditating daily for years now. On some days, my mind is still crazy busy with thoughts popping up like popcorn, and I might find myself thinking about the crud in the dog's ear. On some days, I still express emotion. Just last night, tears rolled down my cheeks during meditation, and sometimes, my session is calm and peaceful. I may even have that goofy grin on my face.

Chapter Twenty-Three

Picture This

All you touch and see is all your life will ever be.

Pink Floyd – Breathe

You're watching a scary movie that you've seen before. When the music gets creepy and the circumstances get tense, your heart starts racing, your breath becomes a shallow pant, and the muscles in your neck tighten up even though you know that everything turns out OK.

Your body reacts similarly all the time to your thoughts, whether make-believe or real and to your benefit or not. The thoughts, words, and images that run through your mind cause constant physical changes in your body. On brain scans, many of the same neurons fired in the brain and neurochemicals were secreted whether an event was being imagined or actually experienced by participants. From a neuroscientific perspective, imagining an act and doing it are not all that different, and both directly influence your physical and emotional states.

Consciously directing this process by visualization, also called guided imagery, causes very real physiologic consequences in your body which you can use to build a better brain and life.

In his book *The Brain That Changes Itself: Stories of Personal Triumph from the Frontiers of Brain Science*, Norman Doidge tells of an experiment in which two groups exercised a finger muscle for four weeks. One group actually did finger contractions while the other group just imagined doing the same thing with a voice shouting at them, like a coach, to work harder. At the end of the study, the first group who had actually done the physical exercises, increased the muscular strength in their fingers by 30% while the other group, who had just visualized, increased their muscle strength by 22%. Doidge explains that during the imaginary contractions, neurons responsible for movements were activated resulting in the increased strength.[1]

He also tells of experiments with amputees who had painful phantom limbs. After twelve weeks of therapy in which they just imagined moving their amputated limbs, some experienced a decrease in pain while the pain completely disappeared in half of them. The visualizations they performed activated and changed brain networks for limbs that weren't even there.

Along with meditation, I visualized daily for years during my recovery from the brain injury as part of what I came to call my "healing time." It was amazing to me that almost everything I seriously spent time visualizing eventually came to be. Coincidence? Maybe. Maybe not. Although the realities didn't materialize nearly as quickly as I wanted them to, better late than never, right? The waiting helped me learn patience.

When I first started visualizing my brain was in pretty bad shape. Because I knew that connectivity overall and getting signals from one side of my brain to the other needed improvement, I would visualize an old telephone switchboard like the one my grandmother operated at a residential hotel in the 1960s. I could see her sitting at the switchboard with her headset on her jet black, pin curled hair plugging the incoming call wires into the holes for the requested room. Similarly, I visualized my brain making the necessary connections to allow the needed communication in my head.

The images naturally evolved as my healing progressed. Next, I imagined my brain finding information via a system like the old, card catalogue files that used to be in place in libraries. Then, I graduated to picturing my brain being able to do a quick Google search.

Visualization is a recognized mind-body therapy that can be effective with any health concern and has proven to be extremely successful in relieving chronic pain, improving performance, changing behavior, or influencing an outcome. Easily used with meditation and other mindfulness practices, visualization is another mental health tool that's always free and available to you everywhere at any time.

Again, there are many good in-depth guides on visualization available. I recommend Shatki Gawain's *Creative Visualization: Use the Power of Your Imagination to Create What You Want in Your Life*. In it, she offers the following guidelines for visualizing: [2]

1. **Set a goal**

Decide specifically something you would like to have, work toward, realize, or create.

2. **Create a clear idea or mental picture or feeling**

This should be in PRESENT TENSE. Think of the situation ALREADY existing and immerse yourself in feeling of it.

3. **Focus on it frequently**

Bring the idea to mind often in quiet meditation or casually throughout your day. Make it part of your reality in a light, relaxed way.

4. **Give it positive energy**

Think about your goal in a positive, encouraging way. See yourself receiving it or achieving it. Feel the feeling of doing that.

When you cut your finger, you don't have to tell your body, step-by-step, the specific details of how to heal the wound – thank goodness! Your body already has the natural wisdom and power to do what's in its best interest. Visualization allows a person to harness and consciously direct this powerful, internal force for healing and other benefit.

While visualization can be effective for many things, I don't know that it is a good use of your time to sit around visualizing winning the lottery. Sorry.

Chapter Twenty-Four

Giving Thanks Changes Your Brain

Gratitude unlocks the fullness of life and turns what we have into enough and more. It turns denial into acceptance, chaos into order, confusion into clarity...it makes sense of our past, brings peace to today, and creates a vision for tomorrow.

Melody Beattie

Now while I don't advocate the butterflies and rainbows sort of positive thinking, research has uncovered some significant benefits to having an attitude of gratitude. Studies show that the practice of gratitude can increase your overall health and happiness levels by 25%.

It may seem like a no brainer (pun intended), but let's talk about what gratitude is exactly. It's a feeling of thankfulness and appreciation; it's reframing your thinking to see the glass as half full instead of half empty; it's viewing a day as partly sunny instead of partly cloudy. Gratitude is a shift in perspective and a conscious choice. In any situation, you can choose a feeling of lack or abundance and a state of complaint or gratitude. Every day, in every circumstance, this choice is always available to you.

At first, it may be difficult to see life from the glass half-full angle and may even feel forced or fake. That's OK. With regular practice over time, being grateful becomes a habit and a default setting which will show up more than just at Thanksgiving. Finding gratitude has become a way of life which helps to keep me positive and motivated.

I began practicing gratitude right after the suicide attempt when I could barely walk, talk, or function. My sons had gone to live in another state, and my future looked pretty bleak. Being appreciative DID feel fake, however the alternative, focusing on all that was wrong in my life, only made me feel worse, bringing more hopelessness and pain. Even though I really had no idea what I was trying to do, expressing gratitude every day for the little things – for the roof over my head, for my dog's companionship, for the money in the bank - did make me feel better and ease my anxiety.

As with meditation, there really is no right or wrong way to practice gratitude. Right is whatever feels right to you. Some activities you might try to cultivate gratitude are:

1. praying

2. writing in a gratitude journal

3. placing a thankful phone call

4. making a daily mental gratitude list

5. writing a thankful letter to someone

6. giving someone or something a compliment

7. stop complaining or gossiping

8. say "thank you" for the big and small stuff

9. celebrate little things

10. look for the lessons, even in the chaos

11. donate your time or money

Gratitude is primarily studied by self-reporting, but for you skeptics, there are increasingly promising results measuring hard scientific data such as cortisol and stress levels, heart rate variability, and brain activation patterns. Some studies are showing how mindfulness practices including gratitude can actually rewire the brain's frontal lobes.

Living with gratitude and mindfulness improves your life. Research has shown that having an attitude of gratitude not only makes you happier, but can also improve your physical health, relationships, emotions, personality, and career. Gratitude can make you more likable, sleep better, exercise more, have more energy, live longer, bounce back quicker, and improve your marriage and career. And it's free!

Chapter Twenty-Five

Forgiveness: The Gift That You Give Yourself

The best way to escape the past is not to avoid or forget it, but to accept and forgive it.

Unknown

Forgiveness is one of those concepts that sounds really admirable and everybody agrees that it's a good thing, but when it comes right down to it, it's not so easy. Thinking of forgiveness as a gift that you give to yourself may make it a little easier. You do it for you, not the other person. The receiving individual doesn't have to deserve it, need it, want it, or even know that you did it for you to reap the benefits.

After my suicide attempt, I had a whole lot of forgiving to do. First of all, I had to forgive myself. That was a hard one. I was mad and disgusted that I was seriously brain injured and that I had DONE IT TO MYSELF! I couldn't even blame it on anyone else no matter how much I wanted to.

As I learned, forgiveness must be extended to yourself before you can give it authentically to anyone else. I started reading everything and anything I could about the act and practicing forgiveness meditations and exercises to offer compassion to myself for the first time in my life. Instead of kicking myself in the behind and criticizing all of my mistakes, I began to talk to and give compassion to myself like I would a friend.

While I certainly considered myself a compassionate person before the injury - I mean was the biggest, bleeding heart around - I realized that my compassion had never included myself. I would forgive anyone in my life for almost anything, no matter how heinous, yet there was never a good enough reason for me not to live up to the high expectations I held for myself.

Having a brain injury actually taught me to have compassion and forgiveness for myself. After the suicide attempt, I walked awkwardly with no grace - think baby giraffe. My hands shook. I couldn't talk understandably. I couldn't eat without spilling food on myself. I couldn't even make it to the bathroom sometimes. If I didn't extend some grace to myself, how could I expect anybody else to do so? I adopted the mantra, "I'm doing the best I can with who I am at the time" which I also applied to my many past screw-ups.

I continued my forgiveness campaign by sending long emails to the major players in my life forgiving them for "whatever I felt like they needed to be forgiven for" and asking for their forgiveness for "whatever they felt like I needed to be forgiven for." The specifics didn't matter on either side. Some people responded with kindness and understanding. Some responded with judgment and "How could you?" I understand both. I didn't need their OK, and it wasn't necessary for forgiveness to take place on my end.

I had honest, open talks with my sons apologizing profusely for being ready to completely abandon them and throwing their lives into a blender and pressing the "ice crush" button. They were forgiving and had some anger understandably. In the coming years, I have a feeling that we're going to have many more talks as they confront their wounds and give words to feelings as they mature. It may not be fun, but I'm prepared to help them heal in any way I can. I know that we are, by no means, finished with this discussion.

As I began to forgive myself and others, I started to feel lighter and happier. It was as if I had set down weights that I didn't even know I'd been lugging around for a long, long time.

Research has shown forgiveness to be positively associated with five markers of health: physical symptoms, medications used, sleep quality, fatigue, and somatic complaints (those pesky things that have no real medical explanation, such as gastrointestinal problems, constipation, nausea, headaches, skin disorders.) Studies have also proven forgiveness to be associated with lower depression symptoms, blood pressure, and heart rate.

Conversely, holding a grudge, harboring hostility, resentment, or anger creates stress in your brain and body which actually shrinks your brain, decreases serotonin levels, and plays a part in almost every disease.

From your brain's perspective, forgiveness requires making a deliberate decision to move beyond feeling hurt or wronged. It takes consciously shifting your perspective and attention, thought reframing, and pairing sad or disappointing memories with more positive, better feeling thoughts. When done repeatedly, over time this practice rewires your brain and builds new neuronal pathways through neuroplasticity which become the default.

Forgiveness may even play a role in healing. Many believe that holding on to unforgiving feelings contributes to the inability to heal. Carolyn Myss, in *Why People Don't Heal and How They Can*, explains that, "Forgiveness frees up the energy necessary for healing."[1] The Buddha said," If we haven't forgiven, we keep creating an identity around our pain, and that is what is reborn." Elizabeth Lesser, in her book *The Seeker's Guide* writes "Humans are just inches away from paradise, but that last inch is as wide as an ocean. That inch is forgiveness." She goes on to say:

> *Forgiveness is an action, not an idea.*
> *We **understand** karma; we **practice** forgiveness. Like any difficult task we undertake, forgiveness requires both understanding and skill. And like any skill, it takes time and practice to strengthen our ability to forgive.*[2]

Forgiveness is a process. Like most of the mental health tools I've covered, it's a practice, a lifestyle, and a gift that keeps on giving to you, your brain, and others.

Chapter Twenty-Six

The Fountain Of Youth For Brain And Body: Exercise

Those who think they have not time for bodily exercise will sooner or later have to find time for illness.

Edward Stanley

Maybe you already exercise to tone your thighs, keep your weight in check, or ward off the major killers, but did you know that moving your body is about the best thing you can do for your brain? Research is showing that physical exercise improves your mood, memory, and learning. While the benefits of a workout have been well-known for your heart for a long time, the incredible advantages for your brain are just being discovered.

So much evidence is accumulating that physical exercise is the miracle potion for getting and keeping your brain healthy at any age. The exact amount or intensity of exercise required has not yet been determined, although it appears that the minimum is thankfully low. Studies have even shown that strength training can have lasting cognitive benefits.

Research confirms that low impact activities with varied movements such as walking, gardening, or swimming have brain benefit. Exercise enhances the connectivity of brain circuits, increases gray matter (actual neurons), combats and even reverses brain shrinkage associated with aging especially in the regions responsible for memory and higher cognition, increases performance on cognitive tasks, and helps shield you from stress and depression.

Moving your body increases the blood flow to your brain which in turn, elevates oxygen levels. The increased blood flow triggers biochemical changes protecting the new resulting neurons by bathing them in nerve growth factor allowing the formation of new neural pathways and connections with neighboring neurons. Because of this, exercise aids learning, and activities requiring you to move and think at the same time, like tennis or ballroom dancing, provide the biggest brain boost.

Just like your muscles, your brain cells need to be stressed to grow and doing complicated activities requiring coordination and thought challenges them and enhances attention and concentration. Researchers found that high school students scored better on tests after doing 10 minutes of a complex fitness routine compared to 10 minutes of random physical activity.

The Alzheimer's Research Center promotes exercise as one of the best weapons against the disease. In addition to the other benefits, exercise protects your hippocampus, which governs memory and spatial navigation, which is one of the first brain regions affected by Alzheimer's. A recent Finnish twin study showed exercise to reduce the risk of dementia even over genetics.

Exercise also reduces stress and anxiety by increasing levels of soothing brain chemicals, like endorphins, serotonin, dopamine, and norepinephrine. Exercise may even work on a cellular level to reverse stress's toll in aging our bodies. Studies found that stressed out women who exercised vigorously for an average of 45 minutes over a three-day period had cells that showed fewer signs of aging compared to women who were stressed and inactive.

Research has also shown that burning off 350 calories three times a week through sustained, sweat-inducing activity can reduce symptoms of depression about as effectively as antidepressants. This may be because exercise appears to stimulate the growth of neurons in certain brain regions damaged by depression. One study found that three sessions of yoga per week boosted participants' levels of the brain chemical GABA, which typically translates into improved mood and decreased anxiety. (I'm a yogaholic!)

Physical exercise was a huge part of my rehabilitation. Once I learned how beneficial it was, my life became all about encouraging neuroplasticity through exercise and putting it to work for me in healing my brain. Self-directed neuroplasticity, guided by exercise and activity, was key to my recovery.

For the first months after the injury, I went to the local Y, working out regularly on the elliptical machine, Stairmaster, or treadmill, and in aerobic classes. Well, I tried to participate as best as I could in the group classes. Because my timing and coordination were way off, I looked down right goofy and wasn't in step. However, by repeatedly challenging my brain and body to do the movements, I forced my brain to make new connections to master the exact things that were difficult for me. I'd sweated regularly my entire adult life motivated by vanity up until that point. Little did I know how well my ego would later serve me.

Upon continuing to learn more about how to better my brain, at 10 months post injury, I began doing cardiovascular activity every day, usually 45 minutes to an hour, but, no less than 30 minutes. Everyday. No excuses. I remember running in the pouring rain and all bundled up in the snow with only my eyes peeping out. When it came to working out, I had a compulsive drive because I desperately wanted to recover and because my brain wasn't functioning optimally so I tended to be OCD.

While I'd aimed this laser beam focus on many things that weren't to my benefit in the past, such as a man or having an immaculate house, my obsessiveness helped me tremendously now. I exercised almost every day for years. At a year post injury, I also added hot yoga to the mix, but didn't count it as exercise. It was my relaxation.

Thankfully, I recovered far beyond what the doctors predicted and enjoyed the added benefit of getting in the best shape of my life, in my late forties no less. Still to this day, exercise and yoga are an important part of my life because they are crucial to maintain my mental and physical health, especially as I age, and because I enjoy them and don't feel right without them anymore.

If exercise can improve my damaged brain, just think of what it can do for a brain suffering from depression or anxiety. Even 10 minutes of activity changes your brain for the better. Get moving!

Chapter Twenty-Seven

Garbage In, Garbage Out

Take care of your body. It's the only place you have to live.

Jim Rohn

When it comes to your brain, you literally are what you eat, drink, and do. The architecture and function of your brain reflects the choices you make every day in your life. Garbage in, garbage out.

Science has discovered that you have a brain in your gut, called the enteric nervous system, and has linked it to many conditions including stress, depression, autism, and even osteoporosis. This finding gives a whole new meaning to the term "gut reaction" and turns out there's some validity to a "gut feeling." Your gut is literally your second brain and is created from the identical tissue as your brain during gestation.

The enteric nervous system consists of a network of some 100 million neurons lining the intestines which is more neurons than are in your spinal cord and can function without any input from the central nervous system and actually sends information to it. While the gut brain is not the seat of conscious thought, it does exert powerful influence on our physical bodies and emotional and mental states. The enteric nervous system uses over 30 neurotransmitters just like the brain above and in fact, your gut brain contains higher levels of the neurotransmitter serotonin, which is strongly associated with mood.

The brain in your head is the biggest energy hog in your body which means it's most affected by what you put in your body. While on average, the brain is only 2% of the body's weight, it uses about 20% of the energy produced. Studies show that a person can be as much as 200% more productive just by making better eating choices. You can promote quicker thinking, better memory and concentration, improved balance and coordination, sharper senses, and the activation of your feel good hormones just by what you put on your plate.

There is plenty of excellent information out there (and debate) about what to eat for optimal brain health. So, I won't go into great depth here, but I'll cover the basics usually agreed upon and cannot stress enough that what you eat has a HUGE impact on your brain, mental and physical health, and happiness.

An intelligent diet would consist of lots of protein, leafy greens, vegetables of all colors, fruit, complex carbohydrates, and good fats. Proteins are the building blocks of the brain and are essential to make neurotransmitters and neurons. Carbohydrates break down into glucose, the brain's primary source of energy. Ideally, you're aiming for a steady supply here.

Simple carbohydrates, processed flour and sugary foods, cause wild fluctuations in blood sugar and can predispose a person to diabetes which leads to a higher risk of Alzheimer's. In fact, there's some evidence that Alzheimer's may be a third type of diabetes of the brain. Riding the blood sugar roller coaster is just not good for any part of your body.

Your brain is more than 60% fat, brain cells are covered by a myelin sheath which is 75% fat, and fats play a crucial role as important messengers in your brain. Your brain needs fat. According to the Mayo Clinic, the risk for cognitive impairment or full-blown dementia is 42% lower in elderly people who eat a diet higher in fat and lower in carbohydrates.

Brain friendly fats would be the omega-3 fatty acids found in such foods as fish, nuts, seeds, and avocados or in a supplement – not the kind found in fried or processed convenience foods. Greens, veggies, and fruit also provide your brain with vitamins, especially the essential Bs, minerals, and antioxidants.

On the flip side, it's equally important to realize that certain foods and substances can diminish your brain power and functioning. For optimum brain health, you want to limit your exposure to and intake of neurotoxins, substances that interfere with the electrical activity of the nervous system. Neurotoxins interact with nerve cells by either overstimulating them to death or interrupting their communication process. You eat and are surrounded by known neurotoxins every day as they are prevalent in our food, water, and environments.

Studies have shown that neurotoxins can shorten the life span of nerve cells and have been linked to brain disorders, neurodegenerative diseases such as Alzheimer's, Huntington's, and Parkinson's, and can cause reactions including migraines, insomnia, asthma, depression, anxiety, aggression, chronic fatigue, and even ALS.

Preferably to avoid neurotoxins and other chemicals, meat should be grass-fed and antibiotic and hormone free while fruits and veggies should be organic. Some of the worst things you can feed your brain would include: excessive alcohol, artificial food colorings, artificial sweeteners, sugars and corn syrup, MSG, hydrogenated fats, fluoride, and nicotine.

Your brain loves water, and it's absolutely essential for optimal brain and body health and function. Water makes up 83% of your blood, the transport system to your brain, making deliveries of nutrients and taking away toxins. Studies have shown that brain cells need twice the energy of other cells in the body, and water provides this, but the brain doesn't have any way to store water.

So, it needs a constant supply, and research also indicates that most people are permanently partially dehydrated. If you're thirsty, you're in this group which means your brain is working below its full potential. Lack of water to the brain can cause problems with focus, memory, brain fatigue and fog, as well as headaches, sleep issues, anger, depression, and more.

Sleep is also absolutely essential to a healthy brain, but it's not because your brain needs time offline, and when you sleep, your brain is surprisingly active. In fact, your neurons fire almost as much when you're asleep as when you're awake.

When you're asleep, your brain is busy with housekeeping and clearing out toxins, making creative connections, and forming and consolidating long-term memories. Healthy sleep is absolutely essential for optimal learning and memory function. A loss of sleep hurts attention, executive function, working memory, mood, quantitative skills, logical reasoning, even motor dexterity, and can literally shrink your brain. The amount of sleep needed varies among individuals and changes with age, gender, pregnancy, puberty, and more.

Napping can give your brain a real boost and make up for any sleep deficit. Taking a nap can make you more attentive and productive, and the 20-minute power nap has been shown to increase alertness and motor learning skills. In one study, a 26-minute nap improved NASA pilots' performance by 34%.

Research reveals that shorter naps help boost memory and enhance creativity while slow-wave sleep, napping for approximately 30 to 60 minutes, is good for decision-making skills. REM (rapid eye movement) sleep, usually 60 to 90 minutes of napping, plays a key role in making new connections in the brain and problem solving.

Living the best life you can, happy and healthy, means adopting a lifestyle supporting your brain's optimal functioning which is directly dependent on what you expose your brain to and feed it. You can't expect your brain to be at its best if you give it crappy nourishment and subject it to all kinds of harmful substances.

If you treat your brain right, it will treat you right.

Chapter Twenty-Eight

Can We Talk?

Courage doesn't happen when you have all the answers. It happens when you are ready to face the questions you have been avoiding your whole life.

Shannon Alder

For the decade before my suicide attempt, I went to mental health counseling on and off. I'd show up for my sessions, spill my guts for an hour, shell out lots of money and, for the most part, get nothing out of it. Throughout all the years, I took antidepressants and was on them when I tried to commit suicide.

Looking back, I realize that the whole process failed miserably because I didn't paint a true picture of the real me for the therapist. Now don't get me wrong. I certainly didn't go in there and say everything was peachy, but I also didn't divulge my deepest, ugliest secrets, habits, and thoughts. You kind of have to be honest for therapy to work.

Scientific evidence shows that cognitive behavioral therapy (CBT), a form of talk therapy, actually works because it takes advantage of neuroplasticity to make physical changes in the brain. CBT is based on the idea of changing your thoughts and feelings to alter your behaviors which recruits different neural networks forming new connections and pathways in your brain, which makes establishing new behaviors easier. Change your brain; change your life.

In their book, *The Winner's Brain: 8 Strategies Great Minds Use to Achieve Success*, Jeff Brown and Mark Fenske explain that CBT was found to be more effective at calming the amygdala, the fear centers of the brain, and curbing emotional overreaction than antidepressants. Unlike the effects of medication, which wear off shortly after stopped, the benefits of CBT last long term.[1]

Under the direction of a licensed clinician, CBT involves a person evaluating their current behaviors to identify strengths and weaknesses – honestly – and decide on specific, measurable goals. Then, they commit to making changes in thinking and behaviors to play up their strengths and limit weaknesses to reach the goals. As we all know, that's the hard part. The new cognitive behavioral skills must be practiced and implemented regularly, over and over, even when it's not easy or fun, in order for the brain to make neuroplastic changes.

CBT is not a quick fix. It can take weeks, months, or even years to replace rigid thought patterns and rewire your brain, but think of how long it took to get those habits etched into your brain in the first place.

Behavioral activation therapy (BAT) is similar to CBT but focuses solely on changing a person's behavior by getting them to do the things that they are likely to find enjoyable, meaningful, or useful, and stop doing things which may contribute to depression. One of the hallmarks of depression is not being able to get any enjoyment out of the activities and events that you used to.

BAT helps turn this around by having a person set goals which they can easily accomplish, and when they do, their brain rewards them. For instance, part of BAT might be as simple as getting up every morning at 7:00, making the bed, and taking a shower. By doing these small tasks, a person is accomplishing little goals which causes their brain to reward them with positive neurochemicals. BAT uses changing the behavior to change the brain via neuroplasticity.

Two years after my suicide attempt, I found an awesome mental health professional who used CBT to help me change my brain and life. This time, I told the truth in all its messy, ugly detail, and found the therapy transformative. Well what do ya know?

I stopped taking my antidepressants and have never felt the need to go back on them. In the years after the brain injury, I assembled what I call my "mental health tool box" filled with the practices explained in this book. It's my antidepressant. One of the best things about my toolbox is that I always have it with me to address whatever pops up and to keep me centered and happy on a daily basis.

I would like to say some words about antidepressants. Whether I'm for them or against them doesn't matter. Each person has to find what works for them. Antidepressants can help treat depression, but come with serious risks, a fact that I think is treated far too casually by prescribing professionals - but untreated depression and psychiatric illness carry significant risks too. Make no mistake about it, whether they work or not, antidepressants are serious drugs affecting the chemistry of the brain. When I tried to commit suicide, I was already on one antidepressant and was two weeks into taking a new one in addition to it.

The truth is that, just as there is a great deal still unknown about how the brain functions, experts aren't really sure how antidepressants work. You might have seen depression explained as a "chemical imbalance" or a "serotonin deficiency." It's not quite that simple. We really don't know what causes depression, how it affects the brain, or what's a cause and what's a symptom.

Many researchers believe that the benefits of antidepressants stem from how they affect brain circuits and brain chemicals that carry signals from one nerve cell to another. In ways not totally understood, different antidepressants affect how these neurotransmitters behave, but there's no test that can measure chemical levels in a living brain and no way to know what a low or normal level is, much less how antidepressants alter these.

Newer research suggests other biological contributors to depression, including inflammation, elevated stress hormones, immune system suppression, abnormal activity in certain parts of the brain, nutritional deficiencies, and shrinking brain cells. And these are just some of the possible biological causes of depression. Social and psychological factors, such as loneliness, lack of exercise, poor diet, and low self-esteem, also play an enormous role in the condition.

Nonetheless you've seen it on ads, read it in articles, and maybe even heard it from your doctor: depression is caused by a chemical imbalance in the brain that medication can correct. People demand the drugs; doctors prescribe them; and insurance pays for it.

Over the past two decades, the use of antidepressants has skyrocketed. One in ten Americans is considered depressed, and among women in their 40s and 50s, the figure shoots to one in four. In 2010, antidepressants were the second most commonly prescribed medication.

According to a research report published in *The Journal of the American Medical Association,* antidepressants work best for very severe cases of depression and have little or no benefit over a placebo in less serious cases. The success rate of antidepressant use is even less outside of clinical trials because of real world conditions such as co-existing illnesses.

Let's look at the stats. If we give one hundred depressed people medication, about thirty people will recover completely within a couple of months. Another twenty will get better, but still feel slightly depressed. And if we give the remaining fifty people a different antidepressant, about fifteen will see improvement and a few more will improve with a third medication.[2]

Research shows that with therapy alone, the numbers are similar to the first round of antidepressants with roughly half of the people showing substantial improvement. If psychotherapy and medication are combined, the chance of recovery almost doubles.

Depression is a complex illness with a basis in brain neurochemicals and thought patterns with many other contributing factors such as life events, environment, physical health factors, and heredity. There's no one-size-fits-all solution. The one right thing is the need for people to be informed about depression, the probable contributing factors, and possible treatments before taking an antidepressant. And when a medication is decided as the way to go, the person needs to be monitored by a professional initially and beyond.

Chapter Twenty-Nine

Depression Treatments You May Not Know About

I did then what I knew how to do. Now that I know better, I do better.

Maya Angelou

Depression looks different in every person, with unique causes, symptoms, and manifestations in that person's brain and life.

For some, breaking a sweat, changing their diet, meditating or writing in a gratitude journal regularly helps. For someone else, medication can jumpstart feeling better. For others, talking with a therapist brings relief. And still for some, a combination of these may work, while nothing seems to help an unfortunate few.

While antidepressants and psychotherapy are the first line treatments for major depression, they don't work for all people. In these instances, alternative therapies may be used instead of, or in addition to, standard treatments. Many practices which treat depression by modifying brain activity, called neuromodulation, have had success. These techniques range from experimental to proven and non-invasive to surgical procedures.

The only way to find what eases depression for any particular person to is to consult a mental health professional and try various treatments until something works.

Transcranial Magnetic Stimulation

Transcranial Magnetic Stimulation (TMS) is a non-invasive procedure which uses magnetic pulses to alter neural activity. During a TMS procedure, a magnetic coil is placed near the head. The coil is connected to a generator and produces small electrical currents in the region of the brain just under the coil via electromagnetic induction. TMS has proven successful in treating major depressive disorder, migraines, symptoms of schizophrenia, and stroke damage.

To simplify greatly, depression is a dysfunction in the communication between the brain's frontal lobe, the thinking brain, and limbic system which controls autonomic bodily functions, particularly in response to emotional stimuli. TMS has been shown to increase dopamine release and help restore better communication and balance between the brain's frontal lobe and limbic system.

Neurofeedback

Neurofeedback is a specialized form of biofeedback therapy, a mind-body technique where people learn to influence their autonomic nervous systems, that focuses on helping a person's brain learn at a subconscious level to permanently alter their own brainwaves. Although it sounds like science-fiction, neurofeedback has been around since the 1950s and is a reputable, scientifically-proven modality practiced by specially-trained psychotherapists.

Neurofeedback is a non-invasive therapy where EEG sensors are placed on the scalp and ears to read the electrical activity of the brain. Brainwaves are monitored by a computer which gives real-time feedback to the person training in the form of an auditory or visual reward, like a video game. The person plays the video game with their brain. With consistent repetition, the brain learns to self-regulate and makes permanent physiological changes to perform more optimally which continues even when not training. Because it's a learning process, the results of neurofeedback occur gradually over time.

Neurofeedback has been used successfully for many conditions including depression, anxiety, autism, ADD and ADHD, brain injuries, stroke recovery, addictions, seizure disorders, learning disabilities, and more. Because neurofeedback fine tunes the brain's performance, it can also be used to heighten focus and concentration such as required for school, playing golf, or other sports.

I started neurofeedback 14 months after my suicide attempt and did it extensively for the next two and a half years. It dramatically contributed to my recovery from the brain injury and may have helped to cure my depression along with it.

After the brain injury, my thoughts and speech were not simultaneous and had a delay in between – if you can even imagine such a nightmare. After just 10 sessions of neurofeedback training, they became simultaneous again, and my sleep became deep and contiguous which I think allowed further healing.

In neurofeedback, we'd train specific areas of my motor strip, and I would feel the corresponding areas of my body waking up with what I came to scientifically call "the tinglies," and those areas would improve. Powerful stuff!

Vagus Nerve Stimulation

Vagus nerve stimulation (VNS) is a surgical procedure that can be used for treatment-resistant depression. A pacemaker-like device about the size of a silver dollar is implanted in the chest and attached to a wire that is threaded along and delivers impulses to the vagus nerve. The vagus nerve travels up the neck to the brain where it connects to areas involved in mood regulation.

VNS was originally developed to treat epilepsy and for reasons not completely understood, these electrical impulses transmitted via the vagus nerve to the brain, affect the neurochemicals, specifically norepinephrine and GABA, and can relieve epilepsy and the symptoms of depression. However, VNS is not a quick answer as it can take several months before the effects are felt.

Electroconvulsive Therapy

Electroconvulsive Therapy (ECT) is a technique in which electricity is delivered to the head causing a brief, therapeutic seizure. ECT got a bad reputation from negative media portrayal, like in *One Flew Over The Cuckoo's Nest*, and because early treatments administered high doses of electricity without anaesthesia, leading to memory loss, fractured bones, and other serious side effects.

ECT was developed in the 1930s when there were few alternatives for treating psychiatric conditions. Since the 1950s, ECT has been performed using anaesthesia, is FDA approved, and has advanced so that there a few side effects.

Like antidepressants, the exact reason ECT works is not fully understood, but it has broad effects on the brain, impacting many neurochemicals and brain cell growth. ECT can quickly treat severe depression, reverse symptoms of certain mental illnesses, and often works when other treatments are unsuccessful.

Transcranial Direct Current Stimulation

Transcanial Direct Current Stimulation (tDCS) is a simple technique using constant, low current delivered to areas of the brain via electrodes on the scalp to either excite or inhibit neuronal activity.

Although tDCS is still an experimental form of neuromodulation and not currently FDA-approved, it potentially has several advantages over other brain stimulation techniques because it's cheap, non-invasive, painless, and safe.

Several studies suggest tDCS may be a valuable tool for the treatment of neuropsychiatric conditions such as depression, anxiety, Parkinson's disease, and chronic pain. Research has also demonstrated cognitive improvement, such as quicker learning and improved memory, in some patients undergoing tDCS.

Deep Brain Stimulation

Deep Brain Stimulation (DBS) involves surgically implanting electrodes in the brain which modify and regulate brain activity. Similar to VNS, a pacemaker-like device is placed in a person's chest with a wire that travels under the skin connected to the electrodes in the brain which controls the amount of stimulation delivered to the electrodes.

DBS is not yet FDA approved, but is currently used to treat a number of neurological conditions including essential tremor, Parkinson's disease, and dystonia, a neurological movement disorder. DBS is being studied for epilepsy, cluster headaches, Tourette's syndrome, chronic pain, and major depression. It has shown potentially dramatic results with depression.

Ultimately, recovering from depression involves altering the brain circuits contributing to the condition which can be done in many ways including lifestyle, behavior, prescription medications, and neuromodulation.

Chapter Thirty

Your Brain Can Be Your Best Friend Or Your Worst Enemy

That's your best friend and your worst enemy - your own brain.

Fred Durst

Your brain can be an ally or enemy in your quest for health and happiness.

With over five million Americans age 65 and older currently living with Alzheimer's and that number projected to triple by 2050, and anxiety disorders being the most common mental illness in the U.S., brain health is up there on almost everybody's priority list - or should be.

An "Alzheimer's pill" isn't likely to make an appearance any time soon. Antidepressant and anti-anxiety medication use is at all-time highs, but everyone is still depressed and stressed to the max. So what's the answer?

Some believe that a diet with lots of fish, blueberries, walnuts, and kale is the panacea. Others are banking on regular physical exercise, a daily Sudoku puzzle, or meditation to be the miracle. While I do highly recommend all of these practices as part of a brain healthy lifestyle, what each of our brains really needs is an individual fitness plan.

According to Dr. Michael Merzenich, co-founder of Posit Science, and author of *Soft-Wired: How the New Science of Brain Plasticity Can Change Your Life*, the answer is right in front of our noses:

> *Contemporary neuroscience has shown us that you come from you. your brain is plastic. You have the power within at any age, to be better, more capable, continuously growing a progressively more interesting life. If you're in decline, you have great resources that can help you sustain — indeed, even regrow — your neurological abilities in ways that can help assure that your active brain shall last as long*

as your physical body. You have powers of re-strengthening, recovery, and re-normalization, even when your brain has suffered large-scale distortions that accompany developmental or psychiatric disorders, and even when it has been physically damaged in any one of the innumerable ways that can befall you in your life.

If you're still alive at the age of age of 50 and you live in the United States or Europe, the average life span extends into the ninth decade of life. Just about every person reading this book can optimistically look forward to living past their 85th birthday. You should know, then, that at that age there is roughly a 50% chance that you will be identified as senile or demented. Other individuals in that cohort will have memory or other impairments that prevent them from sustaining an independent lifestyle. In the latter case, the medical term is 'mild cognitive impairment' (MCI). the only thing mild about it is its name.[1]

The payoffs of adopting brain healthy habits can be enormous for the individual and for our society with the population age 65 and older expected to more than double by 2060 to 92 million according to the U.S. Census Bureau. If something doesn't change, things are only going to get worse – much worse.

Merzenich writes:

Brain fitness is about retaining your vitality, your zest for life, your independence, yourself. It is about giving your brain an excellent opportunity to last as long as your physical body. It's about living longer, alive, full of it, fun, still intense, still confident, independent, still growing, more capable and more interesting next week and next year.[2]

Helping your brain be at its best, which is inevitably going to translate into a calmer, happier you, means making simple changes to incorporate practices like the ones I've outlined here, into your everyday routine. So, what does the bigger brain picture look like?

Suggestions for a brain-healthy life are:

Brain Training

Start spending time doing online brain training consistently at paid or free sites. There are plenty of them available. Certain brain training exercises have been scientifically shown to yield cognitive benefits lasting for years.

Minimize Negative-Learning

Stop or drastically minimize negative behaviors damaging your brain and stressing you out. In addition to the well-known culprits I've already covered, having your daily life constructed to require minimal effort, not asking you to think or pay serious attention, hurts your brain a little more every day. The goal is to challenge your brain often with new experiences and learning. Approaching life with a sense of purpose and curiosity by learning or improving an ability every few months and paying attention and engaging as you go through your daily life - be mindful.

Develop the habit of careful listening and test your memory about what you heard. Study a foreign language. Take a class to learn a new skill, hobby, or art. Learn to play the guitar or dance the salsa. Regularly play ball-in-motion games like tennis, ping-pong, basketball, or Wii games which require you to think and move simultaneously. Play challenging card or board games. Assemble puzzles.

When downtime does present itself, instead of staring at your smart phone or drifting into worry, actively engage your mind with conscious breathing, visualizing, or thought reframing.

Seek And Spread Joy

As your brain becomes calmer and healthier, your life gets a whole lot more enjoyable and you feel happier, which makes your brain even healthier and brighter and the cycle continues. The better it gets, the better it gets!

With conscious practice of the methods I've mentioned, you can build more health and joy into your life and wire your brain for peace and happiness. It is possible with the seemingly small choices you make every day.

Chapter Thirty-One

The Upside of When Things Go South

That which does not kill us, makes us stronger.

Friedrich Nietzche

OK. The shit hit the fan and things got real. (We've all been there, haven't we?) You thought/hoped/prayed the worst of it's over, and you survived! You might be a little bit relieved to know that what doesn't kill you really can make you stronger.

Studies have shown that some trauma survivors report positive changes and enhanced personal development, called post traumatic growth (PTG). PTG can be any beneficial change resulting from a major life crisis or traumatic event, but the most commonly experienced positive shifts are having a renewed appreciation for life, adopting a different world view with new possibilities, feeling more personal strength, experiencing more spiritual satisfaction, and improved relationships.

In the years I spent recovering from my brain injury, I can attest to every single one of these.

There's no standard to determine what constitutes major trauma or healthy growth in somebody. What may be it for one person may be no big deal to another or vice versa, but researchers have figured out why some people experience PTG and some don't.

As expected, it was found that people with a moderate aptitude for psychological adjustment were the most likely to show signs of PTG while those with difficulty adapting experienced less. But surprisingly, people with the highest aptitude for psychological adjustment demonstrated the very least signs of positive change (PTG) maybe because they already understood that difficulty is integral to life, were already adaptable and resilient, and were not that transformed by the challenging experience (which would explain why I experienced such profound growth!)

In the article *How Adversity Can Lead To Happiness* interviewing comedian Jerry Seinfeld, he told of being heckled mercilessly and ignored as a struggling comedian in his early days. On one soul-crushing occasion, people at a New York disco kept right on dancing through his stand-up routine as if he weren't even on the stage. He expressed his belief that his struggles made him a stronger person and better performer.

The article quoted him as saying:

> *I don't mind suffering. You suffer in all things - work, relationships, whatever else you do. Unless you're eating ice cream, you're suffering."* [1]

Victor Frankl, the neurologist, psychiatrist, holocaust survivor, and author, said:

> *The way in which a man accepts his fate and all the suffering it entails, the way in which he takes up his cross, gives him ample opportunity – even under the most difficult circumstances to add a deeper meaning to his life.*[2]

While some pain and suffering in life are unavoidable and just part of the human experience, much of it is self-imposed by our thoughts and can be radically reduced by mindfulness practices and mental health tools, like the ones outlined in this book. Learning to alter my thoughts drastically improved my life and alleviated the self-torture that led to the suicide attempt. To be able to work with the same kinds of challenging situations that used to send me into a panic, and cause such pain and suffering has allowed me to consistently find calm, joy, optimism and trust in myself and the universe.

It's not that I don't have any troubles anymore - far from it, but they don't traumatize me, hijack my life and steal my peace of mind like they used to. After a few minutes, sometimes hours, maybe even days of the "I can't believe this!" feeling, I take a deep breath, stop struggling, and eventually accept what's before me.

Acceptance of the reality that's present is an essential first step to reducing panic, pain, and suffering and to experiencing PTG. To accept doesn't mean to throw up my hands, roll my eyes in exasperation, and say, "I give up." Accept means to stop using my energy resisting or struggling against what is, because doing so only causes me pain and suffering and usually makes things worse. Acceptance means to surrender to the moment as it is, stop focusing on the problem, and start focusing on the solution.

I saw a video by the author and philosopher, Ekhart Tolle. He indicated that people aren't able to surrender until they're completely fed up with suffering. I believe it! He said that a person has to have had enough and, at some level, recognize that the suffering is self-created by their thoughts and that there is another way to live.[3] This was certainly true in my case.

The concept of surrendering is taught in every religion. Surrendering is the central message of Buddhism and is even found in the teachings of Jesus.

Byron Katie writes in *Loving What Is: Four Questions That Can Change Your Life*:

> *The only time we suffer is when we believe a thought that argues with what is. When the mind is perfectly clear, what is is what we want. If you want reality to be different than it is, you might as well try to teach a cat to bark. You can try and try, and in the end the cat will look up at you and say, "meow." Wanting reality to be different than it is is hopeless.*[4]

So, while what doesn't kill you, can make you stronger, you can ease the suffering of going through it by learning to accept what is. Surrendering to any situation isn't going to make it magically go away, but it will make it less painful and hopefully give a deeper meaning and PTG a chance to surface.

If we're lucky, we might even get to the point where we're so evolved we don't even experience PTG anymore.

Chapter Thirty-Two

Focus On The Possibilities Not The Problems

Nothing limits achievement like small thinking; nothing expands possibilities like unleashed imagination.

William Arthur Ward

After the brain injury, I was mentally impaired to the point that I couldn't tell you my phone number or kids' ages, speak understandably, or coordinate the movement of my arms and legs to run. Making a grilled cheese sandwich was an applaud-worthy accomplishment.

My mind wasn't capable of playing the in-living-color, non-stop movies of my brother's sunken eyes and jutting cheekbones before he died of AIDs, me being escorted into my house by a policewoman to get belongings to stay elsewhere because my ex-husband had filed a restraining order against me, or the countless insults his lawyer spewed at me in court as proof that I was a bad wife and mother.

My brain couldn't obsessively question how I could possibly be successful selling real estate when I hadn't worked in a decade and wasn't good with numbers in the first place, or if my boyfriend, who had just broken up with me, had been seeing the woman I found him having dinner with before we split.

All my brain could handle was the right here and right now. Over the coming years as I healed physically and emotionally and slowly came back into consciousness, my brain connected the dots and memories came flooding back along with the capability to think intelligently and reason as well as my old buddies, rumination and worry. My challenge was to hang onto the glimpse of peace, sense of child-like wonder, and ability to exist in the present that the brain injury had shown me.

Who would have thought that an injured brain would lead me to peace?

Being brain injured showed me that the pain which had piled up over the years before the suicide attempt, finally causing me to crumble under its weight, was totally in my thoughts. Yes, the ugly things really did happen – no denying that, but I was the one who kept torturing myself with their memories, forcing myself to relive them over and over again. They were in the past. I could choose to leave them there. I was the one keeping the pain alive and bringing it into my present.

What it really boiled down to was making the decision not to do that to myself anymore. Because of neuroplasticity, the more I dwelled on the hurtful memories, the more I reinforced them because, "Neurons that fire together, wire together." Our brains also add a special subjective sauce to our memories by subconsciously factoring in who you are and what you believe and feel at the time of the recollection. The act of remembering changes a memory. So, as I became more depressed and hopeless, my memories became darker.

But the good news is - and I hope you've learned by now - that the reverse is also true. Neural connections that are relatively inactive wither away, and you can consciously influence the process in a positive, healthier way. I made the memories stronger and more painful, and I could make them weaker and more loving.

The practices I learned as part of rehabilitating my brain, which I've shared with you here, I used diligently to keep my mind from wandering down the slippery slope of darkness and fear that led to the suicide attempt. Every time it started down that road, I'd yank it back with one of my newly acquired tools, and with time and persistence, I rewired my brain.

These days, I remind myself to think of and put energy into the possibilities, not the problems: past, present, or future. This doesn't mean that I ignore reality and live in an illusory world filled with sunshine all the time. It means that I acknowledge and accept what is: both good and bad, consider my possible options, consequences, and outcomes, and choose to focus my energy on creating positive while being prepared to respond (not react) to whatever arises and work with it for my good.

I'd rather take a risk than have regret. Instead of asking "Why?" I ask "Why not?"

In his book, *Just One Thing: Developing a Buddha Brain One Simple Practice at a Time*, Rick Hanson writes:

> *Make room for your dreams in your thoughts and actions. Be their friend. Feel what it would be like if they came true, and how that would be good for you and others.*
> *Without getting bogged down in details or obstructions, give thought to what you could do, in realistic ways, to move toward fulfilment of your dreams. Look for small things you can implement and build on each day...then take action...focus on the things that will make the most difference; put the big rocks in the bucket first.*[1]

I like to call myself a "possibilitarian." If I reach for the moon, I just might land on the stars.

Easy Things You Can Do To Get A Happier Brain Right Now

Happiness is not something ready made. It comes from your own actions.

Dalai Lama

I hope you know, by now, that your happiness or lack thereof is not anybody's fault and there is no blame or shame. It's the product of many different dynamics culminating in certain brain patterns. However, that doesn't mean it's beyond your control.

We've come a long way in the science of happiness and have a pretty good idea of what happy, depression, and anxiety look like in your brain these days. It's now known that what you do in your life every day, because of neuroplasticity, rewires your brain. You can either intentionally direct your brain to become more positive, resilient, and calm or let it get stressed out, anxious, and depressed.

Unfortunately, there isn't a magic pill or one single thing that cures depression and anxiety, or makes your brain calm and happy. Mental strength and having a happy and healthy brain are skills you can learn and support with your lifestyle, the practices I've outlined in this book, and the multitude of small, seemingly insignificant things you do every day.

Your brain is a positive feedback system, and often all it takes is one small shift to keep it feeling good or start it on an upward cycle. While what works for one person may not do any good for another, there are many small things you can try to give your brain a more positive slant to see what works for you.

While no one is happy all the time, staying consistently positive and motivated starts in your brain with routine thoughts, behaviors, and emotions. Small steps can help nudge or keep your brain in a more upbeat cycle and literally start the process of bettering your brain and life right now.

So whether you're depressed, feeling down or anxious, or find yourself in one of those crisis freak-out moments, there are simple steps you can take, backed by neuroscience, right now to start your brain on a more positive path.

If you skipped ahead to this chapter, then all of this stuff will be new to you. If not, here's a quick go-to list, some you've seen before and some new, to help start your brain on an upward spiral right now. These simple practices, worked into your life daily, can make a big difference.

1. **Diaphragm breathing**

   Taking long, deep breaths into your tummy, slows your heart rate and activates the calm, parasympathetic nervous system. Place your hand on your diaphragm, the center of your stomach a couple of inches below your lungs, and take slow, full breaths counting to six, making your hand move in and out with each inhale and exhale. After you get the hang of it, you can practice diaphragmatic breathing anywhere without using your hand.

2. **Stay in the present**

   When you find your mind drifting to the past or future, come back to the right here and now. In this moment, you're OK. It's your thoughts creating the sense of danger. Bringing your awareness back into the now calms the brain's fearful amygdala and engages thinking neural circuits.

3. **Focus on what you can control**

   Avoid imagining the worst possible scenarios, and pay more attention to what is in your control, which modulates brain activity to reduce anxiety.

4. **Zoom out**

   Broaden your perspective, look at the bigger picture, take on different points of view, and try to be objective. Release your emotional investment for a minute. Ask yourself, "Will this matter in a week? A month? A year?"

5. **Make a decision, any decision**

Simply making a decision invokes your thinking brain, increases your dopamine levels, and shifts your brain's perceptual focus to the things that matter the most. Making a decision also elevates your perceived control, giving your confidence and mood a boost which helps propel you to act positively.

6. **Give or get a hug**

A long hug releases the neurotransmitter oxytocin, the bonding hormone, which reduces the reactivity of your amygdala, the fear alarm, and just makes you feel warm and fuzzy.

7. **Get out in the sun**

Bright sunlight helps boost the production of serotonin in your brain. Make an effort to get outside on your lunch hour, go for a walk during the day, or step outside to soak in the sun. Sunlight also improves the release of melatonin which will help you sleep better that night.

8. **Put your feelings on paper**

Writing your emotions down calms your brain and helps you detach and enlist your thinking brain. Or talk it out with a friend or therapist.

9. **Recall some happy memories**

Just remembering good times boosts serotonin in your brain. Try visualizing a joyful memory in detail or write it down.

10. **Visualize**

Use your mind to calm your body by imaging yourself in any setting in which you feel calm and relaxed. Visualize your body and mind letting go of tension. See and feel a good outcome or success or you being able to handle whatever the situation is. (See chapter 23)

11. **Mediate**

Get comfortable and quiet. Observe your thoughts and detach from them while focusing on your breath or a mantra and consciously relaxing your body. Start a daily practice and use meditation in-the-moment when things get intense. You can also practice mindfulness during an activity like running or gardening. (See chapter 22)

12. **View everything as a learning experience**

Whether you lost your cool in a parenting moment, fell short of your goals at work, or spent money you didn't have, adopt a forgiving and learning mindset. Instead of beating yourself up about it, investigate the happening with curiosity. Look for clues as to why you behaved the way you did. What's there to learn? What can you do differently next time to get better results?

13. **Look for the good**

No matter how crappy things are right now, there's always good to be found in your life. There was good in your past, there's good in the present, and there will be good in your future. You have to notice it. (See Chapter 18)

14. **Splash cold water on your face**

Seriously. Find a sink, fill your hands with cold water, and rinse your face. Doing this slows down your heart rate by indirectly stimulating your vagus nerve, which regulates a variety of vital bodily functions including your heartbeat and the muscles used to breathe. The vagus nerve also controls the chemical levels in your digestive system, which greatly affects your mood.

15. Get moving

All forms of exercise, including yoga and walking cause your brain to release feel-good chemicals and give your body a chance to release stress. So, go work up a good sweat, do some yard work, or take a hike in nature. (See chapter 26)

16. Turn on the tunes

Listen to soothing music to calm yourself or blow off some steam and get exercise by dancing around to more upbeat tunes.

17. Get out in nature

Studies have shown that spending time in nature boosts happiness and that if you live close to a green space you're less likely to be depressed. If it's sunny, you get the added benefit of a serotonin increase.

18. Smile or Laugh

It's a simple thing to do and really can improve your mood. Even a fake smile causes your brain to release dopamine. Laughing works for the same reasons smiling does. Think of a fun time, a silly situation or your favorite joke. There's not much difference in your brain between provoked and genuine smiling or laughter.

19. Be around other people

Being with other people, like in a coffee shop, book store, or break room increases serotonin. You don't even have to interact with them. Chatting or chilling with a friend has even more brain benefits.

20. Turn up the heat

Feeling warm can boost oxytocin or at least mimics the effects of it, increasing your feelings of trust and generosity. Wrap your hands around a mug of coffee, cuddle up in a blanket, or take a warm bath or shower.

21. Touch a pet

Just stroking your pet or even someone else's can increase oxytocin, endorphins, and dopamine in your brain. One study showed that playing with a dog with which you have a bond, who is likely to make eye contact with you, increases oxytocin levels.

22. Root for a sports team

Cheering for your favorite team isn't just fun, it makes your brain happy. Cheering for the winning team increases testosterone giving your energy and sex drive a boost. Getting wrapped up in the game also provides a sense of community – even if your team loses.

Resources

Chapter Two
[1]Jonah Lehrer, *Proust Was A Neuroscientist*, (New York, NY, First Mariner Books, 2007), 88-89.
[2] Ibid, 85.

Chapter Three
[1]Alex Korb, *The Upward Spiral: Using Neuroscience to Reverse the Course of Depression, One Small Change at a Time*, (Oakland, CA, New Harbinger Publications Inc, 2015) , 12-13.
[2]Ibid, 30.
[3]Ibid, 13.

Chapter Five
[1]Haara Esteroff Merano, "Depression Doing the Thinking," Psychology Today, https://www.psychologytoday.com/articles/200308/depression-doing-the-thinking, (accessed 5/8/2015).
[2] World Health Organization, "Media Centre Suicide", http://www.who.int/mediacentre/factsheets/fs398/en/, (accessed 6/4/2015).

Chapter Six
[1]Rick Hanson, *Just One Thing: Developing A Buddha Brain One Simple Practice At A Time*, (Oakland, CA, New Harbinger Publications, Inc., 2011), 2-3.

Chapter Seven
[1]Dr. Rick Hanson, *Hardwiring Happiness: The New Brain Science of Contentment, Calm, and Confidence*, (New York, Harmony, 2013), 23.

Chapter Eight
[1]Dr. Dan Siegel, "An Introduction To Mindsight," http://drdansiegel.com/about/mindsight/, (2010).
[2] Dr. Dan Siegel, *Mindsight: The New Science of Personal Transformation*, (New York, Bantam Books, 2010), 55.

[3]Ibid, 54.

Chapter Ten
[1] Alex Korb, *The Upward Spiral: Using Neuroscience to Reverse the Course of Depression, One Small Change at a Time*, (Oakland, CA, New Harbinger Publications Inc, 2015) , 41.

Chapter Eleven
[1]Dr. Robin Berzin, "10 Reasons Why Stress Is The Most Damaging Toxin In Your Life," MindBodyGreen, http://www.mindbodygreen.com/0-14560/10-reasons-why-stress-is-the-most-dangerous-toxin-in-your-life.html, (accessed 5/ 7/2015).

Chapter Twelve
[1] Alex Korb, *The Upward Spiral: Using Neuroscience to Reverse the Course of Depression, One Small Change at a Time*, (Oakland, CA, New Harbinger Publications Inc, 2015) , 65.
[2]Maria Popova, "How Long It Takes To Form A New Habit," Brain Pickings, http://www.brainpickings.org/2014/01/02/how-long-it-takes-to-form-a-new-habit/, (accessed on 5/6/2015).

Chapter Thirteen
[1] Alex Korb, *The Upward Spiral: Using Neuroscience to Reverse the Course of Depression, One Small Change at a Time*, (Oakland, CA, New Harbinger Publications Inc, 2015) , 99.

Chapter Fourteen
[1]J. Loeks, Responding vs. Reacting in Life, http://www.baliadvertiser.biz/articles/mind_up/2009/responding.html, (2009).
[2]Pema Chodron, *The Wisdom Of No Escape And The Path Of Loving-Kindness*, ((Boston, Massachusetts, Shambala Publications, 1991), 1.
[3] Dr. Rick Hanson, *Just One Thing: Developing A Buddha Brain One Simple Practice At A Time*, (Oakland, CA, New Harbinger Publications, Inc., 2011), 197.

Chapter Fifteen
[1]Dr. Dan Siegel, *The Mindful Brain: Reflection and Attunement in the Cultivation of Well-Being*, (New York, New York, W.W. Norton& Company, Inc., 2007) 5.
[2] Ibid, 5.

Chapter Sixteen
[1]Dr· Rick Hanson, *Just One Thing: Developing A Buddha Brain One Simple Practice At A Time*, (Oakland, CA, New Harbinger Publications, Inc., 2011), 174.

Chapter Seventeen
[1]Dr. Rick Hanson, *Buddha's Brain: The Practical Neuroscience of Happiness, Love, and Wisdom*, (Oakland, CA, New Harbinger Publications, Inc, 2009) 96.

Chapter Eighteen
[1]Dr. Rick Hanson, *Hardwiring Happiness: The New Brain Science of Contentment, Calm, and Confidence*, (Oakland, CA, New Harbinger Publications, Inc, 2009), 93.

Chapter Nineteen
[1]Taylor Clark, *Nerve: Poise Under Pressure, Serenity Under Stress, The Brave New Science Of Fear And Cool*, (New York, NY, Little, Brown and Company Hachette Book Group, 2011), 99.

Chapter Twenty
[1]Byron Katie, *Loving What Is: Four Questions That Can Change Your Life*, (New York, NY, Three Rivers Press, 2002), 5.

Chapter Twenty-Two
[1]Osho, "Osho Quotes On Meditation," OSHO, http://www.osho.com/highlights-of-oshos-world/osho-on-meditation-quotes, (accessed on 12/13/14).

Chapter Twenty-Three
[1] Norman Doidge, *The Brain That Changes Itself*, (New York, NY, The Penguin Group, 2007), 316.

[2]Shatki Gawain, *Creative Visualization: Use the Power of Your Imagination to Create What You Want in Your Life*, (Novato, CA, New World Library, 2002) 22-24.

Chapter Twenty-Five
[1]Carolyn Myss PH. D., *Why People Don't Heal and How They Can*, (New York, NY, Three Rivers Press, 1997), 28.
[2] Elizabeth Lesser, *The Seeker's Guide*, (New York, Villard Books, 1999), 362.

Chapter Twenty-Eight
[1] Dr. Jeff Browne and Mark Fenske, *The Winner's Brain: Eight Strategies Great Minds Use To Achieve Success*, (Cambridge, MA, De Capo Press, 2011), 168.
[2]Rush, A.J., Warden, D. et al (2009),STAR *D: Revising conventional wisdom. CNS Drugs, 23(8): 627-647.

Chapter Thirty
[1]Dr. Michael Merzenich, *Soft-Wired: How The New Science Of Brain Plasticity Can Change Your Life,* (San Francisco, CA, Parnassus Publishing, 2013), 5.
[2]Ibid, 251

Chapter Thirty-One
[1]Jordana Divon, "How adversity can lead to happiness," Yahoo News Canada, https://ca.news.yahoo.com/blogs/good-news/adversity-lead-happiness-170812858.html, (accessed on 5/11/2015).
[2] Victor Fankl, *Man's Search For Meaning*, (New York, NY, Washington Square Press, 1985), 88.
[3]Eckhart Tolle, Video of the Day: Eckhart Tolle on How to End Suffering, Intent Blog, http://intentblog.com/video-of-the-day-eckhart-tolle-on-how-to-end-suffering/, (accessed on 5/11/2015).
[4] Bryon Katie, *Loving What Is*, (New York, NY, Three Rivers Press, 2002), 1-2

Chapter Thirty-Two

[1]Dr. Rick Hanson, *Just One Thing: Developing A Buddha Brain One Simple Practice At A Time*, (Oakland, CA, New Harbinger Publications, Inc., 2011), 166.

For more information and inspiration, please visit:

thebestbrainpossible.com

Thank you!

Manufactured by Amazon.ca
Bolton, ON

12836110R00081